Indoor,
Conservatory
and Greenhouse
Gardening

A Wisley Gardening Companion

Indoor, Conservatory and Greenhouse Gardening

ANN BONAR, ALAN TOOGOOD,
DEENAGH GOOLD-ADAMS
and RAY WAITE

Cassell

The Royal Horticultural Society

THE ROYAL HORTICULTURAL SOCIETY

Cassell Educational Limited
Villiers House, 41/47 Strand
London WC2N 5JE
for The Royal Horticultural Society

First published 1994

British Library Cataloguing in Publication Data
A catalogue record for this book is available from the
British Library

ISBN 0–304–32075–7

Photographs by Eden Conservatories (pp. 79, 86), John
Glover, Wilf Halliday/RHS, Photos Horticultural,
Robinsons of Winchester (pp. 74, 78), Harry Smith
Collection, Peter Stiles, Sunrise Conservatories (p. 77),
Technical Blinds (p. 84), Elizabeth Whiting Associates

Line drawings by Mike Shoesmith

Phototypesetting by RGM Associates, Southport
and Litho Link Limited, Welshpool

Printed in Hong Kong by Wing King Tong Co. Ltd.

Cover: Bougainvillea is one of the most luxuriant of climbers
for the greenhouse or conservatory. It thrives in good light
conditions and will tolerate cutting back if it threatens to
overwhelm
Page 2: Anthuriums, with their waxy spathes, make elegant
indoor plants provided they are given warm, relatively humid
conditions out of full sun
    Photographs by John Glover
Page 1: A small greenhouse in spring, the benches packed with
seedlings
Back cover: *Kalanchoe blossfeldiana* flowers spectacularly for at
least two months
    Photographs by Photos Horticultural

Contents

Foreword

It gives me great pleasure to introduce another of the Society's Wisley Gardening Companions. In this volume, three more books in the popular and long-established Wisley Handbook series, *Houseplants*, *Conservatory Gardening* and *The Small Greenhouse*, are brought together under one title.

The joy of owning a greenhouse or conservatory is that it enables keen gardeners to follow their hobby at almost any time, not only when the weather is inclement but even in the dark evenings of winter if lighting is installed. Under glass, seeds can be sown and plants can be propagated in the conditions they require. The young plants can then develop over winter and early spring to give, for instance, a mature display of bedding plants and tender perennials for tubs and baskets as soon as all danger of frost is past. In the same way, a conservatory or greenhouse increases the range of plants which can be grown. They offer protection from frost or rain during winter months to that treasured camellia, citrus or standard fuchsia. In addition, the higher temperatures which can be maintained allow exotics and tropicals to flourish, such as cacti, foliage plants from the rain forests or tender climbers such as bougainvillea and the Chilean bellflower, *Lapageria rosea*.

Houseplants are also very much part of the conservatory and greenhouse scene and, just as important, they are the means of bringing the garden into the home. Many houseplants enjoy the same conditions as we do and there are elegant foliage plants to suit most corners of a house. Winter-flowering plants cheer sunny window sills during the short days, to be replaced by succulents as the temperatures rise.

Glance through the pages of the Companion for more suggestions and advice. There is a very wide range of plants described – established favourites and the more unusual – and in each their care and required conditions are given. So there's no excuse: everyone can garden indoors!

Gordon Rae,
Director General,
The Royal Horticultural Society

Houseplants

ANN BONAR

Busy lizzies, so often a feature of summer patio and
container planting, also make excellent houseplants. The
New Guinea Hybrids have particularly attractive foliage
which can be bronze or variegated

Introduction

Growing houseplants is an absorbing hobby which can be expanded or contracted as you wish and which can take an enormous variety of forms. The range of plants available now is wider than it has ever been and in the modern home, with smoke-less fuel and natural gas, the selection is no longer limited by atmospheric pollution, as it was for the Victorians.

Houseplant cultivation started to become a major hobby during the early part of the last century. The introduction of so many tropical plants from all over the world, to fill the new and fashion-able greenhouses and conservatories being built, resulted inevitably in some of these plants finding their way into domestic homes. Glass cases and special window 'rooms' were constructed for specimen plants or multi-plant displays, in which foliage plants were prominent.

Many of today's plants are easily grown and do not necessarily want high temperatures, though these are much more common with central heating. But what they do need, with very few exceptions, is humidity. A moist atmosphere is as important as water and light, and its lack is a major cause of trouble with houseplants. Unfortunately it can easily be forgotten.

Once you start to grow plants indoors, you will find that you learn a good deal more about their requirements at such close quarters than when cultivating plants in the open. You are more likely to notice insects and diseases and will soon be able to differentiate between a healthy and a sick plant. With experience, a passing glance will remind you that a plant needs watering, whereas to the uninitiated it might appear quite normal.

Whether you are fascinated by large plants towering up to the ceiling, miniature African violets, plants with beautiful leaves or everlasting flowers, bromeliads or ferns, every room in the house can provide a home for some sort of plant and will be enhanced by it. Indeed, a home without plants looks bleak and unfurnished. Houseplants also offer a welcome outlet for frustrated gardeners living in flats.

Hoya carnosa, the wax flower (see p.53), has evening fragrance and is a fast growing climber

Choosing Plants
to Suit the Home

Faced with a large selection of houseplants in a garden centre or shop, it is tempting to buy the one with the prettiest leaves or brightest flowers, take it home and expect it to live happily ever after. But it is much better to consider the conditions in your house first and then choose a plant which matches them in its cultivation needs.

For instance, you may feel that an ideal place for a houseplant is a corner on the landing, which is probably warm in winter but not very well lit at any time. A plant which does not mind shade or a temperature above 60°F (16°C) and is not too fussy about humidity would be suitable, such as mother-in-law's tongue (*Sansevieria trifasciata* 'Laurentii'), sweetheart vine (*Philodendron scandens*) or aspidistra. However, in poor light any flowering plant would gradually fade, become pale and elongated and fall victim to pests and diseases. Similarly, a brightly coloured foliage plant, such as dracaena or codiaeum, would also lose its colour and probably its leaves as well.

By growing the right plant in the right place, you will be half way to successful cultivation. The same applies, of course, if you are given a plant as a present.

TYPES OF HOUSEPLANTS

Until the recent development of numerous flowering plants for the home, the typical houseplant was thought of as a pot plant with ornamental leaves. The variation of leaf shapes among foliage plants is enormous, when you consider the palms, the Swiss cheese plant (*Monstera deliciosa*), ivies, stag's-horn ferns, the umbrella tree (*Schefflera actinophylla*), vines and bromeliads. Add to that a rainbow of colours, from the yellow striping of the spider plant and *Dracaena fragrans* 'Massangeana' to the brilliance of the codiaeums, and who needs flowers? You can have just as striking a display with leafy plants as with flowers and one which lasts all the year round.

Foliage plants, if properly cared for, should reward their owners for several years. Flowering plants, on the other hand, are not quite so easy to grow successfully. Some have a much shorter life, sometimes only a few weeks, and are not intended to be grown for

The large, curiously slashed leaves of the Swiss cheese plant, *Monstera deliciosa* (see p.56)

longer. Cinerarias and chrysanthemums, for example, which bloom continuously and have often been specially treated to enable them to do so, must be regarded as 'throwaway' plants. Even so, they last a great deal longer than a bunch of cut flowers and in that sense give better value for money. Other plants, like the achimenes, the Cape primroses (*Streptocarpus*) and the ever-popular African violets, are especially useful as being both perennial and having a long flowering season.

The size of a plant is an important factor in making your selection – not only its size when you acquire it, but its potential size, together with its rate of growth. It is worth investigating how big a plant will eventually grow, before you buy it, and how fast, remembering that this will determine how often it needs repotting.

ARRANGEMENT AND DISPLAY

The possibilities for showing off houseplants and using them to decorate a home are endless. A windowsill is one of the most obvious places to put them, but be careful if it is south-facing, which can be too hot for many plants. There are numerous special

Browallia speciosa 'Heavenly Bells' (see p.46) is a good plant for hanging baskets

plant stands, including Victorian what-nots, wrought-iron containers on legs and vertical stands with ring attachments for pots, and all kinds of flat surfaces are suitable from tables to bookcases. Open shelving units are an excellent means of displaying plants, especially climbers and trailers, and can act as room dividers.

Hanging baskets, macramé hangers and pot hangers provide a cascade of greenery at different levels without taking up precious space on the floor or on furniture. A well-planted basket looks particularly good near a window and, with the new basket liners and attached saucers, there is no worry about drips after watering.

Climbing plants have great potential and, since many of them tolerate shade, can often be grown in areas of poor light away from windows. They require support and can be trained in various shapes or to go round doorways.

Houseplants grown in groups not only make more of an impact visually, but benefit one another too, because they give off water vapour from the leaves and create a locally humid atmosphere. You should choose plants with similar cultivation requirements for the purpose.

CONTAINERS

Containers are an integral part of any display and, like the plants, are available in a huge variety of designs, shapes and colours. The old, heavy, clay pots have largely given way to plastic pots, often with their own matching drip saucers, and as well as conventional pot shapes, there are squares, cylinders, troughs, urns and hanging baskets. A plain container may be concealed in a larger one of ceramic, plastic, or another material, which does not have drainage holes and therefore protects the surface on which it is stood from drips. But be careful that the inner pot is not left permanently in water as a result. Sometimes, too, these outer containers are not fully waterproof and moisture may gradually seep through the base.

BUYING AND BRINGING HOME

Houseplants may be obtained from garden centres, florists' shops and chain stores, as well as from specialist nurseries. On the whole, the standard is high and you should be able to start with a plant which is in good health, not starved, and free from pest or disease.

Look for plants whose foliage is a good dark green (those with leaves naturally variegated yellow or white generally have the word 'Variegata' or 'Aureomarginata' incorporated in their name, or sometimes 'Maculata' which means spotted). Avoid plants with leaves that are torn or decaying or have brown spots on them, with flowers that are wilting or faded, and with stems that are broken or mottled. Inspect them for pests such as greenfly on the backs of the leaves or clustered round the tips of shoots or even on the flower petals, and watch out particularly for red spider mite and scale insect, as they are very difficult to eradicate (see pp.40 and 41). Dry compost or roots protruding through the drainage holes may indicate that the plant has become weak through neglect and it is wiser not to buy it.

Houseplants may also be purchased at market stalls run by the Women's Institute or Townswomen's Guild; general street markets; village jumble sales and fetes; sales held by horticultural

Fruiting in the winter months, the ornamental capsicum (see p.46) needs a sunny position

clubs and gardening societies; and plant fairs run by various charities, including the National Council for the Conservation of Plants and Gardens. Such outlets are often the source of rare or unusual plants unobtainable from normal commercial suppliers, but the quality is not always so reliable. There is also a risk that the plants may have been left outside too long before being sold.

When bringing a plant home, protect it from draughts and wind, preferably with a polythene bag or sheet, so that it does not lose moisture or become cold. Then keep it in a warm shaded place isolated from other plants for a few days, to prevent possible transmission of pests and diseases. Water well if necessary, repot into fresh compost if it appears cramped for root room, and maintain plenty of humidity (see p.20). When it has settled down and all seems well, move it to its permanent position.

General Care

LIGHT

In the open, plants receive light from all sides during the day, though sometimes it is rather dim, and have unlimited space for their roots to develop and so to absorb water and nutrients. Temperature and the humidity of the atmosphere vary, as does rainfall, and many plants have adapted themselves accordingly.

In a house, by contrast, the environment is almost completely artificial and a plant is wholly dependent on you for its healthy development. There is much less light available and therefore most plants need to be near a window or on a windowsill, though not necessarily in direct sunlight, to receive the maximum amount. However, a south-facing window will be too hot and bright in the summer and the leaves may even be scorched. It is only suitable for cacti, pelargoniums and similar plants which are used to these conditions in their native habitats. Flowering plants and plants with variegated or coloured foliage usually require plenty of light, while plants with dark green foliage are often tolerant of shade and can be placed further from a window, perhaps three or four paces away. Do not move or turn a flowering plant which is covered in buds or these may drop off.

If a plant appears to be suffering from too much or too little light, the answer is simply to find a more suitable position for it. Be careful when watering not to leave large drops on the leaves, as these may cause scorch if hot sun shines through them. Plants can also be damaged if they are grown too close to glass, which sometimes magnifies the rays of the sun.

TEMPERATURE

A winter temperature above 60°F (16°C), which is the average in most homes, will suit the majority of houseplants and many do not thrive below 50°F (10°C). However, some definitely prefer to be cooler when flowering – cyclamen and azaleas, for instance, which are happier at about 55°F (13°C). A few are almost or completely hardy, notably tolmiea, aspidistra and ivy, and will not do well in higher temperatures. These are good for cool situations such as halls, landings and glass porches. In general, the best temperature

19

A mixed group of winter-flowering *Primula obconica* (see p.51), which can be grown from seed sown the preceding spring

range for houseplants is between 50°F and 80°F (10–27°C), with 60° to 75°F (16–21°C) the optimum. A constant temperature, without extreme changes between night and day, and a position free from draughts, should be the aim for all plants. Troubles such as falling or discoloured leaves or dropping buds are easily prevented if these conditions are maintained.

HUMIDITY

Bound up with temperature, and just as important, is humidity. The hotter the atmosphere, the more quickly does the water vapour from the leaves evaporate, and the faster the roots must absorb water from the compost. Much more stress is placed on the plant and, if the atmosphere is dry as well as hot, water is lost even more rapidly.

But a moist atmosphere results in a kind of pillow of water vapour floating just above each leaf and slowing down the activity of the plant. Many houseplants are inhabitants of rain forests and, while it is obviously not possible or desirable to have the equivalent of a tropical downpour at intervals in the living room, humidity can be improved in various ways. Regular overhead misting or spraying with tepid water, ideally several times a day, will benefit most plants, except those with woolly or hairy leaves. Other methods are to place trays of water close to the plants, stand the pots on gravel in saucers of water, or simply grow them in groups (see p.17). It is particularly important to ensure a moist atmosphere in a centrally heated home, especially if the windows are double-glazed, and here a humidifier might be helpful.

Excess humidity is rarely a problem in the home. However, when plants show poor growth, lose their buds or flowers or develop brown leaves, the reason is often that the atmosphere is too dry and the humidity should therefore be increased.

WATERING

When a humid temperature is properly maintained, the need for watering is less. Humidity is just one of the many variables determining how much and how often to give water, quite apart from the individual requirements of the plant concerned. These factors include the size of the pot, the material from which it is made, the type of compost, the rate of growth of the plant and its size, the temperature, the amount of light, and whether the plant is flowering, resting or simply growing.

As a general guide, water when the surface of the compost looks dry, or – another indication of dryness – when the container feels light in weight, especially if filled with peat-based compost. Give enough water to fill the space between the top of the compost and the rim of the pot and pour it on fairly rapidly. Then let it soak through and repeat, allowing the surplus to drain through; empty the saucer under the pot if necessary after about fifteen minutes.

Make sure that the compost never dries out completely during the growing season but, at the same time, do not let it remain wet for long periods. If you are in doubt about when to water, use a moisture meter. This is easy to read, efficient and inexpensive, and can be obtained from garden centres and sundriesmen.

Be careful to water peat-based composts thoroughly, otherwise the centre of the root ball of the plant may dry up completely. One sign that this has happened is when the plant requires much more frequent watering than usual, say every two instead of every five days. It is then difficult to wet right through again, except by immersing the root ball in water and leaving it there until sodden. The same treatment is necessary when the compost has dried up so

Cyclamen require careful watering, with the compost kept just moist (see p.49)

much as to shrink away from the sides of the container, with the result that the water goes straight through the drainage holes without being absorbed.

Always use soft water, either rainwater or boiled water, or water which has been standing a day or two, both for watering and spraying. It should be at room temperature to avoid any shock to the roots. Do not get drops of water on the leaves, particularly hairy ones.

Both under- and over-watering can lead to various disorders and sometimes to the death of plants. Too dry a compost can usually be corrected by more frequent watering or soaking, without undue harm to the plant. However, a compost which is sodden and waterlogged can injure or kill the roots and in severe cases, even if the compost is allowed to dry out, it may be too late to save the plant.

If the compost seems very soggy, heavy or poorly structured and the plant looks unhappy, take it out of the container for a day.

Examine the root ball and remove any roots which are brown or dead, leaving only healthy white ones. Then, depending on the extent of the damage, either return to the original pot and withhold water until the surface of the compost has dried out; or repot in fresh compost, with drainage material at the bottom.

Plants with coloured foliage tend to produce more intense colours if kept slightly dry.

FEEDING

With watering goes feeding. Plants manufacture starches and oxygen in the presence of light through the green tissues of the leaves and stems. But they also need mineral nutrients in the growing medium, in the form of potassium, phosphorus and magnesium and many other elements, which the roots absorb at the same time as moisture.

Modern composts are carefully formulated to provide a balanced blend of both bulky constituents, such as peat or loam, and minerals. These nutrients last for varying lengths of time and only after the plant has used them all up will supplementary feeding with a compound fertilizer be necessary. There are numerous brands available, which have been specially prepared for houseplants to give the correct balance of nutrients. Foliage plants benefit from a high proportion of nitrogen, which promotes leaf and stem growth, and flowering plants from potassium and phosphorus, which are important for flowering. Labels show the percentage of nutrients present in the compound, indicated by the symbols N (nitrogen), K (potassium) and P (phosphorus).

Dry fertilizer may be applied in the form of pellets, tablets or sticks, which are pushed into the compost, or as a powder sprinkled on the surface (be careful not to get it on the leaves). These dissolve when the plant is watered, releasing the fertilizer slowly over a period of several weeks, and usually need to be added only once or twice during the growing season. Liquid feeding, on the other hand, consists of dissolving a small quantity of concentrated fertilizer or fertilizer solution in water, at the dilution rate specified by the manufacturer, and then watering it into the compost. Depending on the maker's instructions, liquid fertilizer is generally given about once a week or fortnight, when the plants are in full growth, which in most cases means April to October. No feeding is required when plants are resting and not actively growing, which normally occurs in winter. Some, such as cyclamen and azaleas, should only be fed after they have finished flowering.

Plants which have become undernourished and lacking in all food materials through neglect will generally recover if they are repotted in fresh compost. This should supply the necessary nutrients. Plants can also be affected by overfeeding, so don't be tempted to use fertilizers as a universal cure.

A shortage or excess of a specific nutrient, such as potassium or nitrogen, may be remedied by increasing or decreasing the amount of the mineral concerned. The condition known as chlorosis often develops on plants growing in alkaline compost, which have been watered with hard tap water. It indicates iron or manganese deficiency and is best dealt with by repotting in acid compost and using soft water.

GROOMING AND TRAINING

Some discreet attention to detail can make your plants look as perfect as other people's. Dead flowers, damaged or yellowing leaves and broken stems should be removed before they rot or fall. Foliage plants in particular should have the leaves washed or sponged regularly to remove dust and spray marks and keep them glossy. Proprietary leaf-cleaning agents may also be used, following the manufacturer's instructions, and some of them incorporate an insecticide as well.

Climbing plants will need to be trained up a support, such as canes, split canes, a plastic frame, a miniature trellis or wires. If they have aerial roots, a moss stick is ideal. This is a pole surrounded with damp sphagnum moss or fibrous peat and bound with wire, or a tube of plastic netting filled with moss or peat. Tie in the stems of climbers as they grow with fillis (soft string) or plastic-covered wire ties, and break off the tips just above a leaf or pair of leaves when they have grown tall enough. Trailing plants can be left to their own devices, but checking their growth in the same way will make them leafier and encourage flowering.

Some plants like *Monstera deliciosa* and *Ficus elastica* 'Decora' can grow so large that they reach the ceiling and become difficult to accommodate. The top of the main stem may be cut back to a convenient height and the sideshoots too may be trimmed, each time making the cut just above a leaf or pair of leaves. (The severed bits can sometimes be used as cuttings; see p.34.)

Alternatively, the size can be controlled in advance by reducing the root ball when repotting in spring. Use a knife to cut round the sides and base of the root ball and slice away about a quarter, which will provide room for fresh compost when the plant is returned to a

Above: Azaleas should not be fed until they have finished flowering (see under *Rhododendron*, p.59)
Below: *Epipremnum aureum* (*Scindapsus aureus*), the devil's ivy, may be trained to a support or allowed to trail (see p.51)

container of the same size. The plant will be stimulated by injury to produce new roots and will have a new supply of food with which to carry on this process.

On variegated plants, cut back any plain green shoot or stem which appears to the point of origin to preserve variegation.

TOOLS

The main tool for working with houseplants is a pair of hands. Other useful implements are an old dinner fork, for breaking up a hard, smooth, compost surface; small and large watering cans; a mister or sprayer and a separate one for pesticides – a pint (half litre) size is convenient; soft string or ties; scissors or secateurs; and either a marked measure or a set of measuring spoons for fertilizers and pesticides. Meters are useful though not essential, for determining water or nutrient content of the compost, available light, humidity and temperature, but they should not be relied on for absolute accuracy. A soil-testing kit, which shows whether compost is acid, neutral or alkaline, might be helpful, particularly for lime-hating plants such as azaleas.

COMPOSTS

Composts for plants in containers are of two types – soil-based and soilless. The soil-based ones consist of a mixture of good soil, i.e. loam, peat and sand, together with nutrients and chalk. The John Innes range of potting composts, which is probably the best known, is made up to a specific formula and comes in three grades numbered 1, 2 and 3, the last two containing respectively twice and three times as much nutrient and chalk as the first. JI No 1 is suitable for small plants in containers of up to 4 inches (10 cm) diameter and also for rooting cuttings; No 2 is for pots of between 4 and 7 inches (10–17.5 cm) and is perhaps the best all-purpose compost; and No 3 is for large plants growing in containers of 7 inches (17.5 cm) or more. A soil-based compost is particularly recommended for vigorous, strong-rooting plants in permanent containers.

The proprietory soilless composts may consist largely of peat, with fine sand but no loam, plus varying amounts of nutrients and chalk depending on the manufacturer. There are also composts, including the JI type, in which the peat is replaced by such ingredients as coir fibre, composted bark and so on. These are conveniently packaged, light to carry and easy to handle. Many of them now incorporate a wetting agent, which makes them easier to rewet if they dry out. A soilless compost is usually preferable for bromeliads and other tree-dwelling plants.

Ericaceous composts, which do not contain lime, are available for acid-loving plants like azaleas and adiantums. There are also composts with extra grit designed for cacti.

POTTING AND REPOTTING

If a plant grows rapidly and the root tips start to emerge from the drainage holes, it should be given a larger container and fresh compost, otherwise it will become stunted and may die. However, some plants flower better if slightly pot-bound and some large permanent plants have to be kept in the same size of container for reasons of space.

To repot, take a pot about 2 inches (5 cm) larger than the previous one and, if it is a clay pot, put a few crocks in the bottom to stop the drainage hole becoming blocked. Then fill the base with a little compost. Knock the old container against the edge of the work surface to loosen the plant, tip it out gently and sit it on top of the new compost. If any long roots have become wound round and round the outside, cut these back to the surface of the root ball, but otherwise do not disturb the plant. Pack compost in down the sides of the pot, firming it round the root ball, until it is level with the top of the root ball, leaving a space for watering of about $\frac{1}{2}$ to 2 inches (1.5–5 cm) below the rim of the container, depending on its size. Water well to soak and settle the compost.

Many permanent plants need repotting each year in spring, just as growth is starting again. Bulbs for Christmas should be potted in early autumn and cacti can be done in early to late summer.

A less laborious alternative to annual repotting is top dressing. A 2-inch (5 cm) layer of the old compost is removed, disturbing the roots as little as possible, and replaced with fresh compost. However, the plant will then require much more feeding than in the previous growing season.

WINTER TREATMENT

Most houseplants rest naturally in winter, from October to March in the northern hemisphere, when light is greatly decreased both in duration and intensity. At the same time, growth is slowed down by lower temperatures and the need for water is thus much reduced. You should in general give enough water to keep the

Above: Plenty of water is necessary for the winter-flowering poinsettia, *Euphorbia pulcherrima* (see p.52)
Below: *Pilea cadierei*, the aluminium plant, (see p.59), needs a minimum winter temperature of 50°F (10°C)

compost just moist, only increasing the amount if a plant shows signs of growing. In other words, continue to adjust the quantity of water as you do in summer, but be prepared to water much less and at longer intervals. Too much water in winter is one of the major causes of death in houseplants.

Regular watering will of course be necessary for the minority of plants which grow in winter, especially flowering plants such as cyclamen.

Too high a temperature during winter can also lead to trouble, as it may force the plant into growth which is weak owing to poor light. This is often when pest infestation becomes rampant. A day-time temperature about 10°F (5°C) above the minimum required for the plant concerned is the most suitable.

HOLIDAYS

Some thought must be given to the care of houseplants when you are away for more than two or three days and can't ask a neighbour or friend to look after them.

In the summer put the plants in a cool but well-lit part of the house and water them thoroughly, or place them in a bath with about $\frac{1}{2}$ inch (1.5 cm) of water in it. Another method is to group them together beneath a large bowl of water and to run lengths of water-absorbent material from this to the compost in each pot. Thick cotton thread, flannel, towelling or capillary matting may be used and will act as a wick supplying water from the reservoir. The plants may be covered with a tent of clear polythene sheeting to keep the air moist and decrease the rate of water absorption, though this will cut down their light. Remove any decaying vegetation first, otherwise it will rapidly infect healthy tissue in the enclosed humid conditions.

An easier solution to the problem is to use self-watering containers. These have a water reservoir in the base and wicks which automatically regulate the supply of water. Or you can reduce the need for watering in advance, by incorporating the special water-absorbent granules now available into the compost when potting.

In winter, the difficulty lies not so much in watering as in the temperature. If the house is not heated, the temperature can easily fall to 40°F (4°C), which is too low for plants of tropical origin. However, if heating can be provided, the temperature should be low enough to reduce the need for watering, but high enough to ensure survival of the plants.

Specialist Care*

CACTI

Cacti make fine houseplants: they do not need a great deal of attention, some have beautiful flowers and they stand up well to central heating. They will also tolerate neglect better than most indoor plants.

They require very good drainage and are best grown in specially prepared compost containing plenty of grit. Generally speaking, except for the Christmas cactus, water in spring, summer and autumn as you would an ordinary houseplant, but in winter keep the compost almost completely dry, watering about once a month. Cacti need all the light you can provide throughout the year and high temperatures in summer, although in winter many of them should be kept at a temperature of about 45°F (7°C). On the whole, the lower the temperature, the drier the compost should be.

Repot mature cacti every two or three years, either in spring or in summer after flowering and feed after flowering in the second and third year. They flower better if slightly short of root room. (See also the Wisley Handbook, *Cacti*.)

BROMELIADS

Bromeliads are a family of plants mostly native to the tropical forests of South America, where they grow high up in the branches and forks of trees, or sometimes on the ground among rocks. They do not absorb food and water from the trees, but simply use them as supports and take in nourishment from the atmosphere and from rotting vegetation. As a result the root system is small.

Most bromeliads consist of a rosette of leaves, flat and star-like or more upright, forming a central funnel in which rainwater collects and from the centre of which come the flowers. The leaves are attractively marked and coloured and the flowers may be brilliant and long-lasting.

They need shallow containers filled with a peat-type compost, or can be made into a bromeliad 'tree'. This is done by binding peat-type material to forks in a dead branch, on which the plants are

*Orchids are not included in this book; see the Wisley Handbook, *Orchids*.

The distinctive, brightly coloured rosettes of the bromeliad *Neoregelia carolinae* 'Tricolor' (see under *Aechmea*, p.43)

placed and secured with twine or plastic-covered wire until they have anchored themselves with the root.

Water is poured into the funnel, which should be kept full in summer and nearly empty in winter, and the compost must be barely moist at all times. Some, like *Aechmea fasciata*, will grow in average humidity, others such as guzmanias require a very moist atmosphere. Feeding is not very important and the plants are happy in good light or a little shade. The temperature should mostly be moderate, 60 to 65°F (16–18°C), but higher while the offsets are forming, at 70°F (21°C) or more. After flowering, the parent plant eventually dies and is replaced by offsets.

BULBS

Spring bulbs can be grown in bulb fibre or, if you want them to flower every year, in standard potting compost. In this case, you will have to feed them with a proprietary fertilizer when flowering has finished and let the leaves turn yellow and die down naturally, in order to supply food to develop the embryo flower. A resting period should follow, usually in July and August, when little or no water is given, after which they can be repotted in fresh compost.

Bulbs which have been prepared for forcing are potted and watered in late August or early September, then put in a dark cool place for about three months to form roots. Once the shoots have emerged, they may be brought indoors to flower within a few weeks. Ordinary compost or bulb fibre can be used, or the bulbs may be grown in bulb glasses with the roots in water. If you want them to flower again after growing in bulb fibre or water, they should be well fed until the leaves die down and planted outside in spring. They are no good for further forcing indoors.

BOTTLE GARDENS

A large clean carboy of green or clear glass is the best container for a bottle garden, but any large bottle or old sweet jar may be used. A tight-fitting bung or stopper, preferably of cork, is essential to prevent evaporation. About five or six plants should be sufficient and planting is easier if you sketch out the arrangement on a sheet of paper first. Small leafy slow-growing plants are recommended. *Pilea cadierei*, maidenhair ferns, small-leaved ivies, *Pteris cretica albolineata*, mosaic plants, *Peperomia caperata*, cryptanthus and small creeping figs would all be good choices.

The growing medium is made up in layers, starting with drainage material such as shingle 1 to 2 inches (2.5–5 cm) deep, then charcoal $\frac{1}{4}$ inch (3 mm) deep, and finally potting compost at least 2 inches (5 cm) deep. Pour each ingredient in turn down a paper funnel into the base of the bottle, spread it out evenly and firm it down with a cotton reel attached to a cane. Make the planting holes and insert the plants with a pair of long-handled tongs or with old dinner forks attached to canes, firming them in with the cotton reel. At the end of planting, water with a long, thin-spouted watering can or tube, directing the water down the sides of the container. Use just enough to moisten the compost, which will not be a greal deal, then put in the bung. If the condensation inside doesn't disappear in a day or two, remove the bung temporarily. If there is no condensation at all, add a little more water. After that, the bottle garden will require virtually no attention, apart from spraying with water about every six months, and it should last several years before the plants become too large.

CONSERVATORIES

Those houseplant owners who are lucky enough to have a glass porch or conservatory can experiment with a much greater select-

Cryptanthus 'Pink Starlight' (see p.49) is one of the prettiest earth-star bromeliads

ion of plants. The extra light means that many more flowering plants may be grown successfully, including bougainvillea, gardenia, plumbago and stephanotis, and bigger plants, for example, camellia and abutilon, can be allowed to develop fully. The second section of this book, pages 71 to 131, contains all the advice you will need to grow these and many more plants, and explores the almost unlimited flexibility of conservatory gardening.

Propagation

PLANTLETS AND OFFSETS

It is always fun to try to increase your own plants. Even if you have never done it before, there is one foolproof method – and that is using plantlets already produced by the parent. The spider plant (*Chlorophytum*) and mother-of-thousands (*Saxifraga stolonifera*) are two which form perfect tiny plants at the ends of long stems, complete with roots. If cut off and planted in 2-inch (5 cm) diameter pots of moist potting compost in spring or summer, they will start to grow at once.

Offsets are miniature plants growing from the base of the parent at soil level. They occur on the urn plant (*Aechmea fasciata*) and daffodils, among others. They can be removed and planted separately in summer or autumn.

DIVISION

Division is another easy method of propagation, used mostly for herbaceous, not woody, houseplants, for instance the Cape primrose (*Streptocarpus*), African violets (*Saintpaulia*) and mother-in-law's tongue (*Sansevieria*). When repotting, you will see that the crown of the plant naturally falls into three or four parts, each with a central rosette. These will form new plants if you cut carefully between them, making sure that each has some roots attached. They should be planted in individual pots at once and will quickly establish and may even flower the same year.

CUTTINGS

Cuttings can be taken from many plants, especially shrubs, trailers and climbers. It is easy to make the cutting itself, but the difficulty comes in supplying the right conditions to encourage it to root.

A cutting usually consists of a short length of stem taken from the top of a new, non-flowering shoot less than a year old. A tip or soft stem cutting, the sort most often used, is 2 to 3 inches (5–7.5 cm) long, generally needs warmth to root and does so quickly in two or three weeks. It is worth taking several cuttings at a time as a precaution and you can also dip the ends of the cuttings in hormone rooting powder. Soft cuttings are most likely to root from

Busy lizzies, *Impatiens* cultivars, are easily increased from tip cuttings (see p.54)

late May to early July, though geraniums are traditionally left until August.

To make a cutting, cut off the tip of the stem just below a leaf joint and remove the lower leaves or pairs of leaves, usually one or two. Make sure that the cut surface is clean, without ragged edges, and if necessary, recut or trim it up with a sharp knife or razor blade. Using a 3 to 3½-inch (7.5–9 cm) pot, fill it with a light potting compost such as JI No 1 or a special cuttings compost, make a hole at the edge with a stick or dibber and insert the cutting to half its length. The cut end must rest securely on the compost and it should be firmed in well so that a gentle tug on a leaf does not loosen it. Put as many cuttings round the edge of the pot as can be fitted in without the leaves touching and water them in. Then place the pot in a propagator with base heating and transparent cover, or

enclose it in a clear plastic bag, blown-up and secured round the rim with an elastic band. Keep out of direct sunlight and maintain a humid atmosphere, by spraying if required, to prevent the leaves losing too much water and drying up before the stem has started to grow roots. All cuttings should be potted as soon as they have been made, except those of cacti which should be left for a few days to form a dry callus on the cut surface. After rooting, pot the cuttings separately in individual pots of a size to take the roots without cramping them.

A few houseplants, including African violets and rex begonias, can be increased by leaf cuttings. (Details of this method are given under the plant concerned in the alphabetical list, pp.43–67.)

SEED

A number of houseplants, such as busy lizzies and coleus, can be raised from seed and in recent years the range has expanded to include pelargoniums and African violets and some exotic new introductions. It is obviously a much less expensive method of obtaining a new houseplant than buying fully grown specimens, and you can be certain that it will be healthy and free from pests and diseases from the start of its life.

Work with a proprietary seed compost or light potting compost; the latter is quite suitable if you are short of time and wish to leave seedlings where they are until a few inches tall. Use small pots or plastic cartons with drainage holes in the base, fill them with compost, lightly firm down and level the surface, and water to moisten. Then sow the seeds thinly and evenly on the surface and cover them with a thin layer of finely sieved compost, firming it gently. Spray the surface with water and place the containers in a heated propagator or an airing cupboard. Temperatures may vary in the range of 65 to 80°F (18–30°C), but most houseplants are tropical and need high temperatures. They should normally be kept dark, covered in black polythene, although some require light for germination. For individual plants, follow the instructions on the seed packet. Once germination has begun, bring the seedlings into the light and make sure that they never run short of water.

Above: Sinningia hybrids, the spectacular gloxinias, can be raised from seed sown from October to March (see p.63)
Below: Rex begonias can be propagated from leaf cuttings (see p.44)

—— Disorders, Diseases and Pests ——

Many of the common troubles of houseplants arise from unsuitable growing conditions, rather than from diseases and pests. The usual symptoms include discoloured foliage, poor growth and lack of flowers – often produced for totally different reasons. However, these disorders are easily remedied by meeting the correct requirements of light, temperature, humidity, watering and feeding, as described on pp.19–29.

Minor outbreaks of a pest or disease can often be controlled without resorting to chemicals. Indeed, pests like red spider mite and whitefly become resistant to pesticides which are used regularly. There is now a variety of predators, parasites, bacteria and fungi available which will eradicate pests naturally, and which obviate the need to use any chemicals at all. The two most well-known and first used are those for whitefly (a parasitic wasp called *Encarsia formosa*) and red spider mite (another mite, *Phytoseiulus persimilis*). Besides these two pests, scale insects, mealybug, green-fly, vine weevil larvae and leafminer are some of the others which can be treated in this way. There are several companies supplying biological controls by mail order, with instructions for use, and names and addresses can be found on p.69.

If chemical controls are necessary, they should be used with caution, particularly when there are children or pets in the house. Some houseplants may be damaged by chemical pesticides. Always follow the manufacturer's instructions. Do not spray in extreme temperatures, bright sunlight or when plants are dry at the roots and avoid spraying open blooms.

DISORDERS

Symptoms	Possible causes
Lower leaves turn yellow and fall	Sudden drop in temperature. Draughts.
Gradual yellowing of leaves, usually starting at bottom, eventually falling; whole plant may die	Overwatering, compost too wet.
Yellow blotches on leaves or leaves completely yellow before falling	Underwatering.

Upper leaves becoming rapidly yellow or bleached between the veins	Chlorosis – manganese or iron deficiency.
Leaves light green or yellow, sometimes orange or red; plant straggly and slow-growing	Shortage of nutrients, particularly nitrogen.
Leaves pale or bleached; plant thin, weak and drawn	Lack of light.
Variegated or coloured leaves lose markings or fade	Lack of light. Reversion, Compost too moist.
Yellow or white rings on leaves, especially achimenes, African violets, gloxinias	Roots chilled by cold water. Water splashes on leaves.

Symptoms	Possible causes
Brown spots on leaves	Overwatering. Overfeeding. Excess sun. Dry fertilizer on leaves. Too cold, for cacti.
Raised corky patches on undersurface of leaves, especially ivy-leaved pelargoniums, peperomias	Oedema or dropsy – from excessive humidity or overwatering (do not remove affected leaves).
Irregular rusty spots becoming sunken, on cacti	Corky scab – from exposure to sunlight, or lack of light and too much humidity.
Leaves brown, particularly at tips and margins	Insufficient humidity. Draughts. Compost too alkaline. Potassium deficiency. Too much sun for shade-loving plants.
Brown patches on leaves before falling	Underwatering.
Large, pale brown patches, later papery, on leaves, especially African violets	Sun scald.
Red patches or streaks on leaves, also on stalks and bulbs, of hippeastrums	Inadequate watering or bulb scale mite.
Leaves fall without discolouring, or sometimes first turn purplish or silver	Draughts. Sudden drop in temperature. Cold water on roots.
Leaves limp, whole plant wilting	Compost dry or too wet.
Buds or flowers drop prematurely	Draughts. Disturbance to plant by moving or turning. Atmosphere dry. Lack of light. Chilling of roots with cold water. Too little water when buds developing, particularly azaleas. Excessive watering.
Failure to flower	Insufficient light and warmth in growing season. Lack of food. Potassium deficiency. Excess of nitrogen, particularly if abundant leafy growth. Plant pruned wrongly and flowering growth cut off. Temperature too high during storing or forcing bulbs. Compost dry when hyacinths kept in dark.

Failure to fruit

Atmosphere dry. Shortage of food, particularly potassium. Compost dry. Temperature too high.

DISEASES

Symptoms

Cause, treatment and prevention

White powdery spots and leaves and sometimes on stems and flowers, especially begonias, African violets

Powdery mildew. Remove badly affected leaves; spray with carbendazim or triforine. Plants which are dry at roots are more susceptible, so keep compost moist.

Greyish-brown fur on leaves and other parts; sometimes many small red or brown spots on petals, especially cyclamen

Grey mould. Remove dead and dying tissues promptly to prevent infection and spray with carbendazim.

Black or brown rotting at base of stems; plant wilting or collapsing

Foot, crown and root rots. Water with Cheshunt compound; in severe cases, remove all dead parts including roots and repot. Use sterilized compost and pots and clean water.

Orange powdery pustules on leaves, mainly undersurfaces, of fuchsias, cinerarias; masses of chocolate-coloured spores, on pelargoniums

Rusts. Remove and burn infected leaves; spray with mancozeb, propiconazole or triforine; in severe cases destroy plant. Avoid splashing leaves with water.

Thickened leaves and swollen buds turning grey, on azaleas

Azalea gall. Pick off and burn galls; spray with mancozeb.

Leaves mottled, blotched or striped with pale green, yellow or black, also distorted; plant stunted and flowers may be malformed or marked

Viruses, e.g. cucumber mosaic, tomato spotted wilt. Destroy any plant with these symptoms.

PESTS

Symptoms

Cause and treatment

Leaves sticky and covered with black sooty patches; tiny transparent spots on undersides; clouds of small white insects fly up when disturbed

Whitefly. When flies visible, spray undersides of leaves with permethrin or insecticidal soap; sponge leaves. Alternative treatment is to introduce the parasitic wasp Encarsia formosa. Early treatment important.

Young leaves yellowing, curling or distorted; foliage sticky, soiled with sooty mould and white cast skins; small black, pink, green or yellowish insects on shoot tips, buds and leaves

Aphids (greenfly). Spray with permethrin or pirimicarb; sponge leaves.

Fine yellowish speckling or greyish tinge on leaves, which may dry up; plant draped in webbing; minute yellowish green or reddish mites present

Red spider mite. Isolate plant; increase humidity and watering and reduce temperature. Spray thoroughly with malathion or dimethoate three times at weekly intervals. Resistant strains common. Most plants susceptible, particularly in summer.

Symptoms

Cause and treatment

Fluffy white blobs on leaves and at stem joints; leaves dull and plant tired-looking. Foliage becomes sticky

Mealybugs; and root mealybugs. Pick off; spray with malathion, or dab insects with methylated spirits.

Small, flat or raised yellowish or dark brown spots on leaves and stems; sticky and sooty patches, especially citrus, ficus and bay

Scale insects. Spray with malathion or pirimiphos-methyl three times at fortnightly intervals; sponge leaves.

Coarse, pale mottling of leaves; small yellow and grey insects which hop off when disturbed; white specks on undersides of leaves

Leafhoppers. Spray with malathion or dimethoate.

Tiny, narrow-bodied black and white or orange insects on leaves; foliage lightly flecked and silvered

Thrips. As for leafhoppers.

Flowers and young leaves distorted; no new growth on plant; microscopic mites on buds and shoot tips, especially cyclamen, begonias and African violets.

Tarsonemid mites. Burn any affected plant. No effective chemical controls.

Sinuous white or beige lines on leaves, especially chrysanthemums, cinerarias

Leafminers. Remove and burn affected leaves at first sight.

Sudden collapse and death of plant; irregular notches in edges of leaves

Vine weevil – soil-dwelling maggots destroying roots and bulbs (adult beetles eat into leaves). Water with pirimiphos-methyl or dust with HCH or use nematode (*Heterorhabditus* ssp.). Particularly active autumn to spring. Control difficult.

Small, greyish-black flies around plant or on surface of compost

Fungus gnats (sciarids), with thin white maggots feeding on decaying organic matter in soil. Remove dead leaves and mix malathion dust into top of compost; control adults with yellow sticky traps. A nuisance but not harmful to established plants.

Tiny white insects hopping on surface of compost and burrowing back

Springtails. Often abundant in peat-based compost and brought out by watering. Entirely harmless.

Large holes in leaves

Slugs and snails. Caterpillars. Earwigs. Pick off by hand.

41

Above: *Achimenes* (left), from tropical America, prefers warm water, hence its common name; *Aphelandra squarrosa* (right) has beautifully striped leaves, with yellow flowers (see p.44)
Below: *Asparagus densiflorus* 'Sprengeri' (left) is ideal for a hanging basket; the popular Reiger begonias (see p.46) were developed in Germany

A Selection of Houseplants

The following list of houseplants is arranged alphabetically by genus, with asterisks to indicate ease of cultivation. Thus: * = easy to grow; ** = moderately easy; *** = temperamental. The abbreviation MWT denotes the minimum winter temperature required.

Botanical names are constantly changing, but as far as possible those which are now considered valid have been given, with cross-references where necessary under the more familiar names.

Achimenes.* The hot-water plant is a delightful bushy, or sometimes trailing plant about 1 ft (30 cm) tall, with masses of open trumpet-shaped flowers from June to November. The most common colours are blue and purple, but pink, white, red and yellow are also available. It grows from small tubers, which should be planted 2 in. (5 cm) apart and ½ in. (1.5 cm) deep in early spring, in a temperature of 65°F (18°C). Keep well lit but out of direct sunlight and water thoroughly – with warm water is said to be best. Support the upright kinds and nip out the tips to keep them bushy. After flowering, dry off the tubers and store them over winter in frost-free conditions, MWT 50°F (10°C).

Adiantum. Some of the prettiest and most delicate ferns are the maidenhairs. *A. capillus-veneris*** has graceful black stems which grow to about 1 ft (30 cm) and then arch over, carrying thin, filmy, triangular leaves, toothed along one edge. It makes a good plant for the bathroom, where it gets the very humid atmosphere essential to it. Another maidenhair, *A. raddianum* 'Fragrantissimum',** is slightly scented. They require a little shade, not too much warmth, about 60–70°F (16–21°C) and moist, acid compost. Draughts and a dry atmosphere result in browning and withering of the leaflets. Increase by division.

Aechmea. Sometimes called the urn plant, *A. fasciata** is a bromeliad with strap-shaped leaves 1 ft (30 cm) long, of grey-green banded with silver. They form a deeply centred rosette, the 'urn' or funnel for water, from the centre of which comes the bright pink flowerhead with small blue flowers in summer, lasting several months. It is easily grown in a peat-type compost; MWT 50°F (10°C). Increase by cutting off the offsets when about 6 in. (15 cm) tall and potting individually in 3-in. (7.5 cm) pots. Each plant flowers only once and then dies.

Other bromeliads needing similar conditions include *Ananas* (pineapple); *Billbergia*; *Neoregelia*; *Vriesea*; and *Guzmania*, although this requires very high humidity.

Agave. The century plant, *A. americana*,* can grow very large indeed, up to 25 ft (7.5 metres) tall in the open, but the form with yellow-edged leaves, 'Marginata', is much smaller and slow-growing. Quite distinct from this is the neat and small *A. victoriae-reginae*,* whose dark green leaves are tipped and edged with white, growing upright in a cluster to about 6 in. (15 cm). Agaves are succulents and store water in their leaves, so the compost can be allowed to dry between waterings for a day or two. In winter, however, water only about once a month and keep cool, MWT 45–50°F (7–10°C). Plenty of light, with sun and average temperatures in summer, are suitable and humidity is not important. Increase by sideshoots, if produced, or by seed.

Aloe. The partridge-breasted aloe, *A. variegata*,* is an attractive succulent. Its upright leaves grow in a rosette and are triangular in cross-section, white-edged and with dark brown bands on a green background; height is about 6 in. (15 cm). *A. humilis** has similarly upright leaves, but in a much looser rosette and toothed and spiny. Both may be treated in the same way as agaves.

Ananas. See under *Aechmea*.

Aphelandra. The zebra plant, *A. squarrosa*,** is a bushy evergreen shrub in its native Brazil. The white-striped leaves need high humidity and it should be frequently watered to maintain the bright yellow flower spikes, appearing in December and January. Height is about 15 in. (38 cm). Draughts result in leaf drop and the temperature should be at least 65°F (18°C), with good light. If cut down after flowering to leave 3 in. (7.5 cm) of stem and rested for a few weeks, the plant will sprout new shoots and can be repotted and grown on (see p.42).

Araucaria. The Norfolk Island pine, *A. heterophylla* (*A. excelsa*),* comes from the Pacific island of that name and is related to the monkey puzzle tree. A graceful, evergreen, upright plant with frond-like shoots and leaves, it is easily grown to 3 ft (90 cm) or more and will tolerate a little shade; MWT 40°F (4°C). Repot in spring. Good humidity will prevent red spider mite, to which it is prone.

Asparagus. The asparagus ferns, *A. densiflorus* 'Sprengeri',* and *A. setaceus* (*A. plumosus*),* are very different in appearance: the first has long, trailing stems with needle-like leaves all along their length, while the second has feathery, triangular leaves and is much used by florists. Both are related to the edible vegetable. Good humidity will prevent leaf fall and some shade is necessary; MWT 40°F (4°C). Water normally. They can be divided for increase and any stems which become straggly cut back to soil level to encourage new growths (see p.42).

Aspidistra. Sometimes known as the cast iron plant, *A. elatior** was popular in Victorian times, often associated with antimacassars and chenille tablecloths. It stands up well to neglect and pollution and will grow in shade. Its handsome evergreen leaves, glossy and gracefully arching, can grow to 18 in. (45 cm) long. There is also a form, 'Variegata', with cream-variegated leaves, which is now almost unobtainable. Brownish purple flowers with fleshy petals, produced directly from the root at soil level, sometimes appear in early spring. Give average watering, wash the leaves occasionally and repot only every three to four years. Dry air will result in brown leaf tips; MWT 40°F (4°C). Increase by removing suckers in spring and potting separately.

Asplenium. The bird's nest fern, *A. nidus*,** inhabits rain forests in Asia and Australia and needs plenty of moisture and warmth. The glossy, light green leaves each form a single blade in a rosette with a central funnel and can grow very large, up to 3 ft (90 cm) long in the wild. A warm bathroom is ideal, as it likes shade and humidity; MWT 60°F (16°C). It can be bound on to peat on a 'raft' (made with short lengths of wood crossing at right angles) or hung from the ceiling in a hanging basket.

Azalea. See *Rhododendron*.

Begonia. This genus is a large and varied one, and it would be quite possible to fill the house with an assortment of begonias, both flowering and foliage kinds, and nothing else.

The rex begonia** hybrids are perhaps the best known of the foliage sorts, with their large richly coloured leaves in purple, plum and magenta, marked with silver and green, or with a green background and yellow, grey and pink. They are bushy plants, slowly growing to about 1 ft (30 cm) and rather more wide (see p.36).

The Iron Cross begonia, *B. masoniana*, has a deep brown cross in the centre of the corrugated green leaves and reaches a similar size. Where space is limited, the eyelash begonia, *B. boweri*, with hairy margins to the leaves, and *B. bowerae*, with green leaves spotted brown, both make good decorative bushy plants, about 8 in.

The elephant-ear begonia, *B. scharffii* (syn. *B. haageana*), is a tall cane begonia grown mainly for its handsome foliage

(20 cm) wide. All these begonias* have rhizomatous roots.

The cane or shrubby begonias* are tall plants to 3 or 4 ft (90–120 cm). The elephant's ear begonia, B. scharffii (B. haageana), has hairy leaves 10 in. (25 cm) long, with crimson undersides and rosy pink flowers in winter (see p.45). B. incarnata 'Metallica' has shiny green leaves and large clusters of pink flowers borne for most of the year. This group has fibrous roots.

The many tuberous hybrids,* with double flowers in summer, have no equal in the gorgeous colouring and shape of the blooms. Most are in single shades, although there are some very pretty fringed kinds with the margins of the petals outlined in a different colour.

The pendula begonias,* with single flowers, are excellent for trailing over the sides of hanging baskets or pots and are also tuberous-rooted. So too is the charming B. sutherlandii,* with slender reddish stems in quantity arching to form a mound, pointed leaves and a profusion of orange flowers all summer and autumn.

The Reiger begonias,** again are superb flowering pot plants, whose large single or small double flowers in beautiful colours appear continuously in summer and winter. Height is about 9 in. (23 cm) with the same spread, but they are 'throwaway' plants and not worth keeping once they have finished flowering (see p.42).

The same applies to the numerous semperflorens hybrids or wax begonias,* with white, pink or red flowers and green or deep wine-red leaves. These flower from June to November and are then discarded. They can be kept going in winter, but usually the light is not sufficient to ensure good colouring or even flowering.

All begonias prefer shade rather than bright light, particularly the leafy ones. They need good humidity, but only moderate watering as too much easily rots the fibrous shoots or tubers. MWT 50°F (10°C) for the foliage and Reiger kinds. With tuberous-rooted sorts, keep the tubers frost-free and dry in winter, start growing in moist peat-type compost at a temperature of 60°F (16°C) in early spring, then pot into compost.

Propagate the rhizomatous begonias by division, the remainder by stem cuttings. Rex begonias can also be increased from leaf cuttings. An entire leaf is removed, cut across the main veins and laid flat on compost, weighted down. It should be kept warm and humid until new plants have formed from the veins. Watch for mildew.

Billbergia. See under *Aechmea*.

Browallia. *B. speciosa** is a pretty plant which is almost smothered in blue, white or lavender, open, trumpet-shaped flowers, continuing for many weeks in spring and summer, or summer and autumn, depending on when the seed is sown. Height is nearly 1 ft (30 cm), with arching stems, and it is a good plant for hanging baskets. Ample light with some sun is required, enough water to keep the soil moist, but not sodden, and cool conditions, around 60°F (16°C). It is an annual, easily grown from seed sown in spring (see p.16).

Calathea. See under *Maranta*.

Campanula. The Italian bellflower, *C. isophylla,** is a native of northern Italy and almost hardy. It produces a profusion of light blue, open, bell flowers 1 in. (2.5 cm) wide, on trailing stems 9 in. (23 cm) long, from July to November. There is also a white form, 'Alba'. It does best in a light, even sunny place, particularly in a hanging basket, and needs daily watering while in flower, as well as deadheading. As it ceases flowering, new shoots appear and the old stems should be removed. The plant is then rested over winter in cool conditions, no more than 46°F (8°C), and repotted in peat-type compost. Increase by division or tip cuttings (see p.47).

Capsicum.** The ornamental capsicums, relatives of the peppers which are the source of cayenne and paprika, have been selected for their appearance rather than their flavour. The fruits are in fact edible, but very hot. They appear in late autumn to mid-winter and are conical, upward-pointing and coloured yellow, red and purple on the same plant, which is bushy and on average 10 in. (25 cm) high and

Left: The apparently indestructible spider plant, *Chlorophytum comosum* 'Variegatum', and (right) *Campanula isophylla*, deservedly a popular houseplant in Britain (see p.46)

wide. Regarded as disposable plants, they need plenty of water and overhead spraying while fruiting, with sun at some time during the day (see p.18).

Ceropegia. Hearts entangled, *C. woodii*,* is an intriguing plant with waterfalls of stems festooned with thick heart-shaped leaves, of dark green covered in white marbling. Given sun or very good light, it will produce tubular flowers in the leaf-joints, of light purple with dark tips, throughout the summer and autumn. Water moderately, keep on the dry side in winter, MWT 45°F (7°C), and repot every second or third year. Cut straggly stems back by half to make them develop sideshoots. It is easily rooted from cuttings.

Chamaedorea. The parlour palm, *C. elegans*,** and other plams, such as *Howea forsteriana* and the pigmy date palm, *Phoenix roebelenii*, can be excellent houseplants. They grow slowly, prefer slight shade, have a graceful habit and require only moderate watering; MWT 50°F (10°C). However, they are prone to infection by scale insect which, because of their many leaflets, is difficult to eradicate. Good humidity will help to prevent this. When young, repot the plants every spring, and after four years or so, repot every two or three years and feed regularly. Brown-tipped leaves may mean too dry an atmosphere or too much lime in the compost.

Chlorophytum. The spider plant, *C. comosum* 'Variegatum',* is aptly named for its long drooping stems ending in plantlets. It is a handsome and easily grown plant, with a rosette of narrowing arching leaves, each 1 ft (30 cm) long, striped yellow or white down the centre. Good light ensures good leaf variegation; MWT 40°F (4°C). Small white flowers may also be produced in the summer, separately or with the plantlets. It grows rapidly and needs frequent repotting and watering, which will also prevent the leaf tips turning brown. Increase by cutting off and potting the plantlets.

Cineraria. See *Pericallis*.

Cissus. The kangaroo vine, *C. antarctica*,* is native to Australia. It attaches itself to a support by tendrils and has evergreen leaves which are toothed, glossy and shaped like beech leaves, only a little larger. It grows about 6–12 in. (15–30 cm) a year and

Left: *Codiaeum variegatum pictum*, the croton, known also as Joseph's coat, and (right) the enchanting mosaic plant, *Fittonia verschaffeltii argyroneura*, is unfortunately quite difficult to grow

---

makes an attractive well-clothed climber. Preferring cool conditions and a little shade, it is ideal for north-facing windows, halls, landings and corners of unheated rooms; MWT 40°F (4°C). Moderate watering and a humid atmosphere prevent the leaves discolouring and withering.

The grape ivy, *C. rhombifolia,** often confused with *Rhoicissus rhomboidea*, comes from Natal in South Africa. It climbs rapidly by means of tendrils 12 ft (3.6 m), but if pinched back will become somewhat bushy, and has glossy, diamond-shaped, toothed leaves. The cultivar 'Ellen Danica' is more graceful and less tall, with deeply cut and toothed lobed leaves. They do best in a little shade, too much light making the leaves yellowish green, with plenty of water, average humidity and some form of support; MWT 45°F (7°C).

Increase both by tip cuttings rooted in a temperature of 70°F (21°C).

×**Citrofortunella**. The calamondin, ×*C. microcarpa,** is a charming miniature orange tree, with diminutive fruits about 1 in. (2.5 cm) in diameter to match. These are edible but bitter and make good marmalade. An evergreen plant, it grows 12 to 18 in. (30–45 cm) tall and has fragrant white flowers in spring. The oranges begin to ripen in late summer. It needs a sunny place and can go outside in summer. It also requires humidity from overhead spraying, which will help the flowers set fruit. Water moderately and feed while growing, then keep dryish in winter, MWT 50°F (10°C). Increase by tip cuttings rooted in a temperature of 75°F (24°C). Watch for scale.

Codiaeum. The croton, *C. variegatum pictum,** is not a new houseplant by any means and, after its introduction from Polynesia in 1863, numerous hybrids were developed which adorned many Victorian homes. They are highly decorative, with evergreen leaves in yellow, pink, green, orange, red, white and brown, often having four colours on one leaf in blotches and stripes. But they are temperamental. They need steady high temperatures, preferably about 70°F (21°C), no draughts, a very moist atmosphere and frequent watering, together with good light and weekly feeding; MWT 60°F (16°C). Watch for scale insect and red spider mite; leaf drop indicates lack of water, dry air or draughts and pale leaves mean too little light.

Cordyline.** This genus of shrubs and trees from Australasia and eastern Asia is notable for the colourful foliage, in a range of pink, red, magenta, purple and cream flushed pink, on a green background. As houseplants, the leaves are 6 to 12 in. (15–30 cm) long, on a central stem 2 to 3 ft (60–90 cm) high. Plenty of water, good humidity and ample light provide healthy plants; MWT 55°F (13°C). Leaf drop is due to dry air or too little water, poor colour to lack of light. Increase by offsets.

Cryptanthus.* The earth stars or starfish bromeliads, species of *Cryptanthus*, are dwarf bromeliads. Their evergreen leaves are coloured and marked in green, silver, brown, magenta, grey, rose-pink and white, depending on the species or variety, and are 6 to 12 in. (15–30 cm) long, mostly in the form of flattened rosettes. A peat-type compost and good light and humidity are all they need; MWT 50°F (10°C). Water and feed as for bromeliads generally. Increase by plantlets (see p.33).

Ctenanthe. See under *Maranta*.

Cyclamen.*** These are very popular flowering plants, especially at Christmas time, with the reflexed petals of their pink, white, red, crimson or magenta flowers and, even when these have faded, the decorative white-marbled leaves. The new 'mini' cyclamen, only about 5 in. (12.5 cm) high and sometimes fragrant, are a delightful addition to the enormous range available. Cool temperatures of around 55–60°F (13–16°C) while growing and flowering, careful watering and frequent overhead misting are essential to success and will prevent wilting and red spider mite infestation. Yellowing leaves indicate too much water or draughts. Water from the top or bottom, but do not splash the leaves or stems and make sure the compost drains well. After flowering, feed and water until the leaves die down naturally and keep quite dry in a warm place until July. Then, as new growth starts, repot in fresh acid compost, half burying the corm, water moderately at first and shade for some of the day. The plant can be put outdoors until September. Once it is growing well, begin liquid feeding until the buds show, then stop until after flowering (see p.22).

Cyperus. The name umbrella plant is applied to *C. involucratus*,* the more common species, growing to 4 ft (1.2 m), and to *C. albostriatus*, 1 to 2 ft (30–60 cm) high. The stems carry a crown of narrow leaves, fanning out like the spokes of an umbrella, particularly effective in *C. variegatus*, with white-striped leaves. They are thirsty plants, best grown in pots placed in saucers of water, constantly topped up and never allowed to dry out. Otherwise, they are not choosy and thrive in shade or good light and some humidity; MWT 50°F (10°C). Increase by division in spring (see p.51).

Dendranthema.* Pot chrysanthemums are now sold as flowering plants all the year round. They have been treated chemically to restrict the height to about 1 ft (30 cm) and pinched out to produce many sprays of flowers, which last for some two months. While in bloom, they should be watered well and given good light and a temperature of 50–60°F (10–16°C). After that, they can either be discarded or, having removed the dead flowers, they can be repotted into larger containers and fresh compost, when they will return to their natural height of 2 to 3 ft (60–90 cm). They can also be planted outdoors, but will not survive the winter.

Dieffenbachia.*** Commonly known as dumb cane, because the leaves are said to cause blisters on the tongue if eaten, these are handsome foliage plants, but very poisonous. They have fleshy stems 5 ft (1.5 m) high in favourable environments and large 9-in. (23 cm) long leaves, heavily spotted and marked with cream or white. Forms of *D. maculata* (*D. picta*) are the chief ones grown, such as 'Exotica' and 'Marianne', the latter with only the edge of the leaf green. Humidity and plenty of light, but not summer sun, keep the leaves in good condition. Draughts or low winter temperatures will result in leaf drop and dry air in brown leaf edges. If the leaves fall, cut the main stem back to a few inches and it will sprout sideshoots. Water normally in summer, moderately in winter, MWT 60°F (16°C). Increase by suckers, or use the top few inches of stem as a cutting and root in plenty of warmth, 75–80°F (24–27°C).

Epiphyllum 'Cherubim', the water lily cactus, is a forest cactus which flowers in spring

Cyperus involucratus (syn. *C. alternifolius*) (see p.49) is from Madagascar, where it inhabits bogs in the wild; its container should stand in a saucer of water

Dracaena.*** Yet another genus of fine foliage houseplants, the dracaenas show considerable variation from one to the other. *D. sanderiana* is an upright plant with narrow, grey-green leaves edged in white sheathing the stem; it produces sideshoots. *D. surculosa* (*D. godseffiana*) is a low-growing shrubby species, whose dark green, oval leaves are spotted lavishly with cream. *D. marginata* 'Tricolor' has a trunk 4 to 5 ft (1.2–1.5 m) tall, with a rosette at the top of arching, very narrow leaves 15 in. (38 cm) long, striped in green, cream and rose-pink. *D. fragrans* 'Massangeana' has a large rosette of glossy, broad, arching leaves sprouting from ground level, each striped widely down the centre with yellow. Treat as for codiaeums.

Epiphyllum.** These cacti are epiphytic or tree-dwelling, like the bromeliads, and perch on rotting vegetation in the forks of trees. The hybrids grown today, known as orchid or water lily cacti, have exquisitely beautiful flowers in white, pink, yellow, red or salmon, appearing in May to June and sometimes again in autumn. Height is 1 to 2 ft (30–60 cm) and they need supporting with stakes and ties. Water well when the whole compost is nearly dry, keep in good light with sun in winter, supply average humidity and repot every two to three years. In winter they should be allowed to rest in cool dry conditions, MWT 40°F (4°C), without drying out completely. Cut one or two of the oldest stems down to the base if flowering poorly. Increase by tip cuttings in summer or by seed (see p.50 and p.62).

Epipremnum. The devil's ivy, *E. aureum* (*Scindapsus aureus*)** from the Solomon Islands, is a fleshy-stemmed twining plant with strikingly variegated leaves, much splashed and spotted with yellow. The cultivar 'Marble Queen' is so heavily variegated as to be virtually a white-leaved plant and 'Golden Queen' is a similar form but in deep yellow. Both grow more slowly than the species. Small aerial roots are produced from the stems and, if trained into a moss stick, this will lead to larger leaves. Water well while growing and supply plenty of humidity. The species prefers a little shade, but not too much otherwise it becomes plain green, while the cultivars should have good light to retain their variegation; MWT 50°F (10°C). Use a peat-type compost and increase by potting up side stems from the base which have already rooted (see p.25).

Episcia.*** The flame violets, as they are called, are small ground-covering plants with oval, often quilted leaves, picked out in light green along the veins, and red or orange-red flowers. Their requirements are similar to *Fittonia* (see p.55).

Euphorbia. The poinsettia, *E. pulcherrima*,** is very popular at Christmas time with its striking red 'petals'. These are in fact bracts, crowning the top of each shoot to form a bushy plant up to 2 ft (60 cm) tall. New varieties have white, pink or crimson bracts on short plants 9 to 12 in. (23–30 cm) high. Flowers can last until May, during which time the poinsettia needs plenty of water, an even temperature of at least 60°F (16°C) and copious misting, together with good light. Afterwards, it can either be discarded, or the stems may be cut down to a few inches and the plant repotted. New shoots will appear and, to encourage the development of red or coloured bracts, keep the plant in complete darkness for fourteen hours each night during October and November, then allow it natural daylengths (see p.28).

Exacum. The Persian violet, *E. affine*,* is a 'throwaway' flowering plant, but so neat, floriferous and easy to look after that it is well worth having in the house for the summer. It lives up to its namesake too, as it is heavily fragrant. About 6 in. (15 cm) high, it is covered in light purple, gold-centred flowers from June to October. Good light and frequent misting, together with normal watering, will keep it growing well and faded flowers should be removed to ensure continuous blooming. It is easily raised from seed sown in late summer or early spring in a temperature of 65°F (16°C).

× **Fatshedera**. An elegant tall shrub, × *F. lizei** is grown for its evergreen leaves, which resemble very large, well-lobed, ivy leaves and betray its hybrid parentage (it is a cross between *Fatsia* and *Hedera* or ivy). There is also a variegated form with cream tips to the leaves, which is more decorative but less easy to grow. It is partially climbing and requires staking or other support, reaching 6 ft (1.8 m) or more. Almost hardy, it prefers cool temperatures and a little shade, but more light for the variegated form, with average watering and humidity. Increase from cuttings in midsummer.

Fatsia. One of the parents of the above, *F. japonica** has large, lobed, evergreen leaves and is a tall bushy plant. It has the same cultivation needs.

Ficus. The popular rubber plant, *F. elastica* 'Decora',* makes a handsome upright plant with its large, glossy, oval leaves and grows easily and rapidly, reaching the ceiling of many homes. Other members of the genus are equally attractive. *F. deltoidea* (*F. diversifolia*)* is a small, slow-growing, bushy species, with rounded triangular leaves and small yellow fruits like marbles. It is sometimes known as the mistletoe fig. *F. pumila* (*F. repens*),** the creeping fig, has trailing stems clothed in small dark green leaves and can be allowed to trail or be trained as a climber. *F. benjamina*,* the weeping fig, grows into a graceful small tree up to 6 ft (2 m) high, with arching shoots and pointed glossy leaves.

For the last three species good humidity is important, otherwise the leaves fall. The rubber plant needs regular leaf-cleaning and all like temperatures above 50°F (10°C). Water moderately in summer, but less in winter. A little shade suits the small species, while some sun is advisable for the tree-like kinds. Repot every other year and increase by cuttings. Watch for scale insect and red spider mite.

Fittonia. The mosaic plant, *F. verschaffeltii argyroneura*,*** is a native of Peruvian rain forests and has creeping stems, with delicate white netting on dark green leaves. The miniature form, *F. verschaffeltii argyroneura* 'Nana', is easier to grow and particularly suitable for bottle gardens. High humidity, some shade and a good deal of water in summer are necessary for fittonias. In winter water sparingly, MWT 55°F (13°C), although for *F. verschaffeltii argyroneura* 'Nana' 45°F (7°C) is satisfactory. Keep away from draughts. Increase from cuttings of the rooted trailing stems (see p.48).

Fuchsia.* Among the most delightful of flowering plants, fuchsias take kindly to container cultivation and indoor growing. Coolish conditions in summer, in slight shade or good light but not full sun, frost-free in winter and moderate watering are all they ask. There are many beautiful hybrids, single and double flowered, bushy and trailing. (For further details, see the Wisley Handbook, *Fuchsias*.)

Gloxinia. See *Sinningia*.

Grevillea. The Australian silk oak, *G. robusta,** is an evergreen tree 165 ft (50 m) tall in its native land. In the home it is a graceful upright plant, growing quite quickly to 10 ft (3 m) high if well suited, with feathery frond-like leaves. It requires average watering, feeding and humidity, and good light but shade from bright sun in summer. Keep cool in winter, MWT 45°F (7°C), and repot each spring (see p.55).

Guzmania. See under *Aechmea*.

Hedera.* The ivies are universally popular for their attractive leaf shape and colouring and for their habit, which enables them to be grown as climbers or trailers. The small-leaved forms of the common ivy, *H. helix*, vary enormously from plain green to variegated or speckled in cream, yellow or white, grey-green or flushed with pink, alone or in combination. Some good varieties are 'Goldheart' ('Jubilee'), with a golden centre; 'Luzii', speckled light green; 'Glacier', grey-green and cream; 'Eva', with white margins; 'Sagittifolia', with a long narrow central lobe; and 'Buttercup', with pale yellow young leaves. An attractive large-leaved ivy is *H. algeriensis* 'Gloire de Marengo', which has irregular grey-green and cream mottling and red stems. Cool temperatures suit ivies best, some humidity, as hot dry air encourages red spider mites and withering leaves, good light for the variegated kinds and moderate watering. They are easily increased from stem cuttings pinned down flat on the compost surface.

Hibiscus. The hybrids of *H. rosa-sinensis*** make extremely pretty pot plants, bearing large funnel-shaped flowers of pink, red or orange in summer and autumn. The variety 'Cooperi', with leaves variegated cream and pink to deep red, is attractive even when not in bloom. Height is about 2 ft (60 cm), though 6 ft (1.8 m) is possible, and width 18 in. (45 cm). Plenty of warmth, light and humidity are necessary all year, ample water in summer and feeding from early June until September. Prune hard after flowering or in early spring, cutting back shoots by half or more; MWT 55°F (13°C). Increase by tip cuttings rooted in a temperature of 75°F (24°C) (see p.55).

Hippeastrum.** The amaryllis, as it is commonly known, is correctly a *Hippeastrum* hybrid and should not be confused with *Amaryllis belladonna*, quite a different plant. It has trumpet-shaped flowers 6 in. (15 cm) wide at the mouth, carried singly or severally at the top of the stem, in white or shades of red and pink, and strap-shaped leaves emerging from the large bulb. Plants are potted from January to March or earlier in individual 6-in. (15 cm) diameter pots, burying only half the bulb in the compost and watering in well. Keep in a temperature of 70°F (21°C) and water sparingly until growth is obvious, then moderately. Give good light for flowering. Remove dead flowers and feed until leaves die down, then dry off in temperatures no lower than 40°F (4°C) until time to repot again in January.

Howea (Howeia). See under *Chamaedorea* (and also p.56).

Hoya. An easily grown evergreen climber, which may be trained into various shapes, is the wax flower, *H. carnosa.** It will bloom in the second year from a stem cutting, the stiff clusters of pink wax-like flowers, each with a drop of nectar, appearing in summer and smelling sweetly in the evening and at night. Moderate watering, less in winter, and good light, are required; MWT 50°F (10°C). Owing to its fast growth, it should be repotted while young or fed with a high potash fertilizer. Lack of food, hard water or too much water produce yellow leaves (see p.12).

Hypoestes. The polka dot plant, *H. phyllostachya** (long wrongly identified as *H. sanguinolenta*), has been much improved by selection in recent years and the unusual pink spots and blotches covering much of the dark green leaves make it as colourful as a flowering plant: 'Splash' is a particularly good form. The stronger the light, the better the colours, provided the leaves are not scorched. Height is 6 to 12 in. (15–30 cm) and it likes plenty of water while growing; MWT 50°F (10°C). Keep it bushy by pinching out the tips of shoots and use these for cuttings. Scale insect can be a major problem.

Impatiens. The busy lizzie, *I. walleriana** and its progeny, can be very busy indeed, profusely flowering all year if allowed to. But it is one of those plants which should be made to rest by lowering the winter temperature and decreasing the amount of water and light. All flower colours except blue are available, together with cream-variegated or crimson-green leaves and, in the most recent New Guinea Hybrids, green, yellow, red and bronze colourings. Plenty of water and a very humid atmosphere prevent buds, flowers and leaves dropping and ward off red spider mite. A sunny position and temperature of 75°F (24°C) maximum, MWT 50°F (10°C), are further aids to health. Pinch out the tips for bushier, more floriferous plants and root these in compost or water for increase (see p.35).

Jasminum. The jasmine, *J. officinale*,* must be one of the most sweetly scented flowering plants, with white flowers appearing all summer. A rampant climber, it needs a large container and plenty of wall space, but is otherwise easy to grow, being almost completely hardy. Water and feed well in summer, supply good light and humidity and repot in the growing season. Prune in early spring to fit its space.

J. polyanthum* flowers in winter from December to March, in a temperature of 60°F (16°C) or more, and needs ample light and warmth in summer to ripen the new growth. Increase both by division or cuttings.

Justicia. The shrimp plant, *J. brandegeana*,* is one of the easiest houseplants and will flower all year if allowed to. The 2-in. (5 cm) long flower heads consist of overlapping salmon-pink bracts, with tubular, purple-spotted, white flowers protruding from them, on a bushy evergreen plant. In its native Mexico it grows 3 ft (90 cm) tall. Feed in summer, but stop in autumn and keep on the dry side, MWT 50°F (10°C), to allow to rest. Cut it back in early spring by half and repot. Increase from tip cuttings. Watch for red spider mite.

Kalanchoe. The succulent *K. blossfeldiana** has rosettes of rounded fleshy leaves at ground level, from which come slender flowering stems, topped with clusters of small tubular flowers in red, yellow, orange or white. Mostly seen at Christmas, it is in fact available in flower at any time. From 12–18 in. (30–45 cm) high, there are also dwarf versions, about 6 in. (15 cm) tall, while the new Swiss hybrids, with much larger flowers, are 6 to 12 in. (15–30 cm) in height. Let the compost become almost dry between waterings, give good light and average humidity; MWT 50°F (10°C). After flowering, remove the stems, keep the plant nearly dry for several wseeks and slightly shaded, then repot and treat normally. Increase from seed (see p.58).

Maranta.*** The prayer plants, varieties of *M. leuconeura*, are beautiful but demanding small foliage plants, with colourfully marked and often velvety-looking leaves. *M. leuconeura kerchoveana* has brown splodges on the grey-green leaves and *M.l.leuconeura* (*M.l.massangeana*) white veining on a dark olive-green background; *M. l. erythroneura* (*M. tricolor*) has red veining.They need a lot of humidity, high steady temperatures of 60–70°F (15–21°C) and a little shade in summer, but good light in winter, MWT 50°F (10°C). Lack of humidity is the greatest drawback, causing leaf browning and withering very quickly. The use of acid compost and soft water at room temperature are important; do not allow them to dry out. Increase by division (see p.58).

Above: *Episcia cupreata* (left), from South America, likes a very humid atmosphere (see p.52); the lovely *Hibiscus rosa-sinensis* (right) belongs to the same family as mallow and hollyhock (see p.53)
Below: *Grevillea robusta* (left) is grown for its attractive fern-like foliage (see p.53); the hippeastrum (right) is now a popular Christmas present (see p.53)

Howeia forsterana comes from Lord Howe Island in the South Pacific (see under *Chamaedorea*, p.47)

Calatheas and ctenanthes are similar to marantas in general colouring, but up to twice the size, at 2 to 3 ft (60–90 cm) high, and more difficult, as they need even greater humidity.

Monstera. The Swiss cheese plant, *M. deliciosa* (*M. pertusa*),** is a striking and magnificent plant with large leaves, at least 15 in. (38 cm) long and nearly as wide, which are pierced and serrated. Naturally a climbing plant with aerial roots, it grows rapidly to 6 ft (1.8 m) and should be trained on to a moss stick, which is kept moist by spraying; if it gets too tall, cut the top off and root it as a cutting. Some shade, good humidity and a temperature of 65°F (18°C), with watering at sufficient intervals to allow the compost to dry out somewhat, will suit it; MWT 50°F (10°C). If holes and slashes do not develop on the new leaves, some aspect of its care is wrong. Moving the plant to a completely different position will often put matters right (see p.15).

Neoregelia. See under *Aechmea* (and p.31).

Nephrolepis. The ladder fern, *N. exaltata*,* is a fast-growing elegant fern from tropical regions, but will nevertheless stand comparatively low temperatures, down to 50°F (10°C). Its light green, arching fronds are deeply cut into feathery segments and a well-grown plant can be 6 ft (1.8 m) wide, though it will be less in the average pot or hanging basket. There are several attractive cultivars which grow less rapidly. Provide plenty of humidity and acid compost and feed frequently. Increase by runners, pegging these into compost and then potting the plantlets separately (see p.58).

Passiflora. The passion flower, *P. caerulea*,* is a vigorous climber with remarkable blue, white and purple flowers, which are shortlived but produced in quantity between July and September. The plant grows rapidly and attaches itself by tendrils. It requires as much light as possible, plenty of water while growing, average humidity and normal summer temperatures, MWT 40°F (4°C). In a conservatory it may produce edible but rather insipid fruit. In spring cut it back hard and repot. Propagate from seed or by cuttings.

Pelargonium.* Pelargoniums are excellent good-tempered houseplants, mostly flowering freely and continuously all year if allowed to. Zonal pelargoniums – the plants most commonly called geraniums and often used for bedding – have a dark band on the upper surface of the leaves and clusters of small flowers. Regal pelargoniums have funnel-shaped frilly flowers, three or four in a loose cluster. Ivy-leaved geraniums are trailing, with fleshy pointed-lobed leaves, sometimes mottled white as in 'The Crocodile', or variegated grey-green, white and pink, with white flowers, as in 'L'Elégante'. Scented-leaved geraniums have pungent, finely dissected leaves, smelling of lemon, eucalyptus, apple, rose, or sandalwood. The miniatures grow to only about 8 in. (20 cm) and often have brightly coloured leaves as well as brilliant flowers.

Suitable for sunny windowsills, even at midday in summer, the pelargoniums do not need humidity, but require regular watering and drying out between applications. Cut the regals back in summer after flowering and repot them after a rest at this time. Pinch back stems of others to keep the plants bushy and cut back hard in early spring, as growth starts again with regular watering. In winter, keep frost-free and almost dry. Increase by tip cuttings in late summer, or the new F_1 hybrids from seed sown in heat in January or February. Watch for whitefly on regals and rust and red spider mite on all. (See also the Wisley Handbook, *Pelargoniums*.)

Peperomia. There are a number of different peperomias, mostly with attractive leaves, but the best known and least difficult to grow is *P. caperata*,** with corrugated, dark green, heart-shaped leaves about 2 in. (5 cm) long and unusual hooked spikes of white flowers on reddish stems. A small bushy plant to about 8 in. (20 cm) tall, it is neat and slow-growing. It needs plenty of humidity and without this will drop its leaves quickly. Water moderately in summer, less in winter and keep in good light; MWT 55°F (13°C). Increase by leaf cuttings, as for *Saintpaulia*.

Pericallis. The cinerarias are colourful hybrids grouped under the name *P. × hybrida*,* mainly derived from *P. cruenta* and *P. lanata*. Available in winter as flowering pot plants, they are disposable, but their profusion of daisy flowers in bright blue, white, magenta, salmon, pink or wine make them well worth growing, especially as they remain in bloom for at least six weeks. Depending on the type, height can vary from 9 to 24 in. (23–60 cm). A cool temperature, about 50–60°F (10–16°C), is important as they wilt easily. Good light, but not sun, and some humidity are also needed, together with careful watering to keep the compost moist but not waterlogged. Watch for greenfly.

The string of beads, *P. rowleyanus*,* is an interesting oddity. The common name describes it exactly, as the leaves have been converted to solid round balls about $\frac{1}{4}$ in. (6 mm) in diameter, spaced at intervals along the thread-like stems, which trail or form mats of vegetation. It has fragrant purple and white flowers in autumn. As a succulent, it should be watered moderately in summer, about once a month in winter, with plenty of light and average humidity; MWT 40°F (4°C).

Philodendron. The sweetheart vine, *P. scandens*,* owes its name to the pointed heart-shaped leaves, 6 to 12 in. (15–30 cm) long when full grown, with a glossy surface. It is a climber, twining round its support with fleshy stems, and amenable to

Above: *Kalanchoe blossfeldiana* (left) does well on a sunny windowsill; marantas (right) and their relatives need a high humidity (see p.54)
Below: *Nephrolepis exaltata* (see p.56) can be propagated from runners at any time of year

shade; MWT 50°F (10°C). Grow as a trailer or train the aerial roots round a moist moss stick, and water well in summer, moderately in winter. High humidity is important. Increase by cuttings in a temperature of 74°F (24°C).

Phoenix. See under *Chamaedorea*.

Pilea. The aluminium plant, *P. cadieri,** belongs to the same plant family as the stinging nettle. Its 3-in. (7.5 cm) long oval leaves are patched and banded with silver, giving them a metallic gleam and accounting for its common name. Height is about 12 in. (30 cm), though a newer form, 'Minima', is more compact and does not become straggly with age. *P. involucrata* is quite a different colour, with bronze-green corrugated leaves. Pileas need plenty of humidity to avoid leaf drop, moderate watering and good light; MWT 50°F (10°C). Pinch back the stems to keep them bushy. Increase by tip cuttings (see p.28).

Platycerium. The stag's horn fern, *P. bifurcatum,** is an epiphyte, living in trees and rooting into vegetable debris which collects in the branches. From tropical regions, it needs plenty of humidity to maintain its softly hairy, forked, antler-like fronds in good condition. These are the fertile spore-bearing fronds, whereas the thin, rounded, plate-like, green 'leaves', which turn brown and papery, are sterile fronds and act eventually as an anchor, sheathing their support. It is happiest in a hanging basket or attached to tree bark; MWT 50°F (10°C). Grow in a peat-based compost and water moderately.

Primula.* The primulas – *P. obconica*, the fragrant *P. malacoides* or fairy primrose, and the smaller *P. sinensis* – are pretty flowering pot plants to cheer up the winter and easily grown. They last in flower from December to the end of March or even longer, provided faded blooms are removed, pink, blue, mauve, yellow, white and red being the usual colours. Keep them well watered, humid, in good light and cool, at 55–60°F (13–16°C); high temperatures or dry air will encourage red spider mite. *P. malacoides* is usually shortlived, but *P. sinensis* and *P. obconica* may be potted in fresh compost and put outside in a cool place with a little shade until autumn, then brought in and again kept in low temperatures (see p.20 and p.60).

Pteris. The generic name of the ribbon fern, *P. cretica,*** comes from the Greek word *pteron*, meaning a feather. The feathery quality of the fronds is emphasized in the form *albolineata*, which has all its veins marked in white, making it doubly attractive. Growing 12–18 in. (30–45 cm) high, the plant should be given shade, plenty of humidity, acid compost and soft water; MWT 50°F (10°C).

Rhipsalidopsis. See under *Schlumbergera*.

Rhododendron.** The azaleas grown as winter-flowering pot plants are mainly derived from the Chinese R. *simsii*. Their glamorous frilled flowers may be pink, red, white, salmon, crimson and all shades of these, usually very double, and are carried on a small evergreen shrub. When flowering in mid-winter, they need watering daily, sometimes twice daily, and frequent overhead spraying, otherwise the leaves will drop and the plants become infested with red spider mite. A well ventilated but moist atmosphere and temperature of 55–60°F (13–16°C) are best, with ample light but not direct sun. Lower temperatures prolong flowering. Soft water and acid compost are essential. After flowering, cut back all shoots by one eighth of their length to encourage the growth of new shoots for flowering next winter, pot into a slightly larger pot, using ericaceous or acid compost, and put outdoors in a lightly shaded place when the risk of frost is past. Feed every two weeks from that time and remember to keep the plant watered. In September bring it in, stop feeding and water sparingly. The warmer indoor temperature will encourage flower buds to appear and watering should then be increased (see p.25).

Rhoicissus. See under *Cissus*.

Saintpaulia. The much loved African violet, *S. ionatha,*** is now so greatly hybridized that all shades of purple, blue, pink, crimson, white and magenta can be found, together with coloured-edged and double flowers. Miniature and trailing

Above: *Primula malacoides* (see p.59) is treated as an annual but is very free-flowering
Below: 'Tricolor', a diminutive form of *Saxifraga stolonifera*, appreciates bright light

kinds are also available, as well as the normal compact rosette-forming plants. Given plenty of light, but shade from strong sun, they flower all year and most profusely in summer. A steady draught-free temperature of 60°F (16°C) and water given at the same temperature will suit them. Peat-based compost is preferable, kept moist but never sodden, and watering should be infrequent. Humidity is very important, although the hairy leaves should not be misted or sprayed as they can be damaged. Increase by leaf cuttings, by removing a leaf with the stalk attached; push it into damp compost to about half the length of the stalk and keep in a humid atmosphere. Plants can also be increased by division or seed.

Sansevieria. Mother-in-law's tongue, S. *trifasciata*,* comes from tropical Africa and Asia. Its cultivar 'Laurentii', the one grown as a houseplant, has stiff, upright, fleshy leaves, narrowly edged with yellow, about 15 in. (38 cm) tall. With sufficient warmth and light, it will produce a fragrant white flower spike. Water moderately in summer, sparingly in winter, MWT 50°F (10°C). Too much water and too low a temperature in winter result in the stems rotting at soil level. Increase by division.

Saxifraga. Mother of thousands, S. *stolonifera*,* is so named for its ability to produce plantlets at the end of thread-like stems hanging from the central rosette of leaves. The leaf colouring is dark green veined with white, with an undersurface of crimson, and delicate, yellow-centred, white flowers are produced in airy clusters on 12-in. (30 cm) stems in May and June. The very attractive form 'Tricolor' has white-edged leaves, flushed pink, but needs a higher temperature and is less easy to grow. The species itself is nearly hardy and does best in a temperature of 50–60°F (10–16°C), with a little shade or good light and moderate watering and humidity. Increase by potting the plantlets individually.

Schefflera. The false aralia, S. *elegantissima*,*** hails from Australasia and is an elegant upright plant with narrow, dark olive-green leaflets much serrated at the edges, carried in clusters of seven to ten. It is slow-growing to about 5 ft (1.5 m) in twelve years, but can be temperamental, readily shedding its leaves as a result of draughts, dry air, cold or fluctuating temperatures. Plenty of humidity, an even warm temperature of 60°F (16°C) or more, and compost at a similar temperature are vital. Keep in good light, repot at two- to three-year intervals when mature and feed occasionally. Watch for red spider mite and scale insect.

The umbrella tree, S. *actinophylla*,* is grown for its evergreen leaves, which consist of about seven drooping leaflets radiating from the leaf stem, the whole leaf being about 9 in. (12 cm) wide. It is good-tempered and does not require a good deal of warmth, accepting a temperature of about 50°F (10°C) in winter, or lower for short periods if kept on the dry side. Water freely in summer, sparingly in winter and place in good light or a little shade. Height is about 6 ft (1.8 m) in the home, though in its native Australia it can grow to 130 ft (40 m), and pinching out the growing tip will encouraging branching. Watch for red spider mite and scale insect. Increase by stem cuttings, which need a temperature of 75°F (24°C) in the compost.

Schlumbergera. The Christmas cactus, with the awkward botanical name of *Schlumbergera* × *buckleyi** (formerly *Zygocactus truncatus*), is a profusely flowering plant from November until January. The bright magenta-pink flowers look like fuchsia blooms with protruding stamens and are produced at the end of flattened stems, which are divided into segments and have scalloped margins. It is an epiphytic or tree-dwelling cactus and grows in the same conditions as the brome-liads. A peat-type compost is advisable to start with, repotting in a soil-based kind as it matures, for it becomes very large, 2 ft (60 cm) and more across. Water moderately while flowering, give good light and spray overhead occasionally in a centrally heated room. After flowering, water sparingly and lower the temperature to 45–50°F (7–10°C) to allow it to rest. Repot annually in spring when young, every third year when mature, and put outside in light shade until September, when it should be taken back indoors. New shoots appear in midsummer and buds in

October, so long as it is given the short daylengths normal in autumn. By keeping the temperature down to about 55°F (13°C), it is possible to delay flowering until Christmas, but the duration of this treatment will depend on individual plants.

The Easter cactus, *Rhipsalidopsis gaertneri,** needs the same cultivation conditions, except that its resting period is September to December rather than February to April; it should also receive natural daylengths in the autumn. Winter temperature should be about 65°F (18°C) and the buds appear from February.

Increase these cacti by cuttings of two to three stem segments, allowed to dry a day or two, in late spring or summer. Watch for mealy bug and root aphids; prone to bud drop.

Scindapsus. See *Epipremnum*.

Sedum. *S. sieboldii** is a succulent, with toothed round blue-grey leaves in pairs along its hanging stems. The whole plant grows to about 10 in. (25 cm) wide and from September to November bears heads of tiny purple-pink flowers. There is also a form, 'Mediovariegatum', which has an irregular creamy-yellow stripe to each leaf and grows more slowly. Easily cultivated, this sedum will stand winter temperatures down to 35°F (2°C) or 45°F (7°C) for the cultivar, especially if kept on the dry side. In summer it needs sunlight or plenty of light and moderate watering. The leaves turn purple in late autumn and can last well into winter, but the plant then dies back completely. Repot in spring and divide for increase.

Sinningia.* The gloxinias or *Sinningia* hybrids have some of the most beautiful flowers among pot plants. Large, velvety and trumpet-shaped, 3 in. (7.5 cm) wide, there are as many as twelve on one plant, lasting for about two months and set off by green leaves up to 10 in. (25 cm) long. Height is 9 in. (23 cm) and colours are red, purple, pink, white and blue-mauve, with the Tiger race having spotting on the throat. They need shade from strong sunlight, plenty of water while growing, average summer temperatures and some humidity. After flowering, dry off gradually in the autumn and keep the tubers at about 50°F (10°C). In spring repot and do not water until the leaves appear. Depending on their flowering time, between June and August, they are potted from March to May. They can be raised from seed, sown at intervals in warmth, to bloom through the year (see p.36 and p.65).

Solanum. The winter cherry, *S. pseudocapsicastrum,*** belongs to the same genus as the tomato and potato. The small round bright red fruits are the size of marbles, scattered all over a bushy little plant about 9 in. (23 cm) tall. It is a 'throwaway' plant, available in early winter. To make sure it does not drop its fruits and leaves as soon as you get it, give it plenty of humidity by spraying at least once a day and put it with other plants. Place in good light and water well; MWT 55°F (13°C).

Solenostemon. The flame nettle or coleus, *S. scutellarioides,** usually grown in the form of its hybrids, is valued for its brilliant gaily coloured leaves, which far outdo the many insignificant flowers in their effect. Unfortunately, in Britain they are short-term plants for the summer and autumn and in the poor light of winter their leaves fade to an anonymous beige. The leaves may be heavily fringed and toothed, even jagged, at the edges, and ruffled, while the colour combinations are dazzling. Average height is about 2 ft (60 cm), but in optimum conditions – overhead light, plenty of warmth and water and good compost – they will grow to 4 ft (1.2 m) tall and 2 ft (60 cm) wide. Pinch out the tips of shoots to keep them short and bushy, and remove flower spikes. Increase from seed sown in spring in 60–70°F (16–21°C).

Streptocarpus.* This may sound like an illness, but it is the generic name for the Cape primrose. These beautiful flowering plants from South Africa have funnel-shaped flowers with smooth or trilly petals, 1½–2½ in. (4–6 cm) wide, in clusters on

A brilliantly-flowering collection of mixed cactus includes epiphyllum (above), rhipsalidopsis (left), aporocactus (right) and chamaecereus (below)

The Cape primroses (*Streptocarpus* hybrids) are easily grown in cool temperatures

stems averaging 9 in. (23 cm) tall. The blue 'Constant Nymph' is the one generally grown. The Concorde group is especially pretty in a range of blue, lilac, purple and white and the Royal race has larger flowers; some kinds have dark pencilling in the throats. They flower from June to November or longer. Good light but not sun, ample water while flowering, much less in winter, and some humidity are factors in successful growing; MWT 45°F (7°C). Plants grow quickly and need feeding during the growing season. Increase by division in spring and repot annually.

Syngonium. Like the philodendrons and monsteras, S. *podophyllum** is a member of the arum family and is commonly known as the goosefoot plant, from the shape of the young leaves. The fleshy climbing stems produce aerial roots, so a moss stick is an ideal support. Cultivars with variegated leaves include 'Emerald Gem', with yellow veining; 'Emerald Gem Variegated', whitish leaves with variegations; 'Silver Knight', silvery green leaves. Lots of humidity is essential; MWT 60°F (16°C). Normal watering, provided the compost does not start to dry out, and a good light for the variegated kinds, a little shade for the plain-leaved ones, will result in healthy plants. Increase from stem cuttings (see p.65).

Thunbergia. Black-eyed Susan, T. *alata*,* is an annual climber, with flat, orange, brown-black centred flowers 2 in. (5 cm) wide all summer on a plant some 6 ft (2 m) tall, though it can be kept shorter and bushier by pinching out the tips and restricting the pot size. There are yellow- and white-flowered forms as well. Keep well watered and in bright light with some sun and average humidity. Discard old plants in autumn and grow from seed sown in a temperature of 65–75°F (18–25°C).

Tolmiea. The piggyback plant, T. *menziesii*,* is so named from its habit, unique among houseplants, of producing plantlets on the upper surface of the leaves where these join the leaf-stalks. It forms a bushy plant about 6 in. (15 cm) tall, of pleasant light green, and is very tolerant, except of heat and dry air. There is also a variegated form called 'Taff's Gold'. It is nearly hardy, so does best in cool temperatures, MWT 40°F (4°C), with plenty of water and average humidity and good light or a little shade. It is very easy to increase from plantlets.

Above: Gloxinias are descended from a Brazilian species, *Sinningia speciosa* (see p.63)
Below: *Syngonium podophyllum* 'Emerald Gem' does best in a well-lit position

Tradescantia should be given good light to preserve the leaf colours

Tradescantia.* The name Wandering Jew covers several genera, but the trades-cantias are the best known, plants with trailing jointed stems to 3 ft (90 cm) and pointed oval leaves in pairs, striped white or light yellow. *T. fluminensis* is the plain green-leafed one; *T. fluminensis* 'Argenteo-variegata' has yellow markings on the leaves and *T. fluminensis* 'Tricolor Minima' has pink, green and white leaves, flushed red beneath. If stems get straggly, cut them back hard and repot the plant. *T. albiflora* 'Albovittata' is altogether larger, with thicker stems and larger, more obviously striped leaves. White flowers may be produced. Water well in summer, sparingly in winter, supply good light and feed while growing; MWT 45°F (7°C). Increase by tip cuttings in summer (see p.58).

The purple heart, *T. pallida* 'Purple Heart' (*Setcreasea purpurea*),* from Mexico, is a stiffly trailing plant used for ground-cover in the tropics. Its fleshy jointed stems are sheathed in narrow pointed leaves, both having an overall colour of deep purple, and in late summer it produces tiny purple-pink flowers. It grows vigorously in high temperatures and bright light, but fades in poor light. Plenty of water in summer and a moderate amount in winter will keep it healthy; MWT 50°F (10°C). The stem tips

The darkly blotched foliage of *Begonia* 'Tiger Paws' provides colour all year round

can be pinched out to encourage sideshoots and used as cuttings, which root easily in summer.

*T. zebrina pendula*** is striped dark green and silvery green with a purple underside. *T. zebrina* 'Quadricolor' has white added to these, all flushed purple and with a purple underside. *T. zebrina* 'Purpusii' is coloured in varying shades of purple. They are exceedingly attractive trailers, though slow-growing to about 1 ft (30 cm). Give plenty of light and water moderately, less in winter, MWT 50°F (10°C). Too much food makes them a uniform green.

Vriesea. See under *Aechmea*.

Yucca. Although it may seem an unlikely plant to grow indoors, *Y. elephantipes*** is widely available, either as a foliage pot plant with a short trunk and cluster of leaves at the top, or as a dormant plant called a ti tree or happy plant. The ti cane – a piece of dried woody stem or cane – is planted vertically, or horizontally half-covered, in moist peat-type compost. With a temperature of 65–70°F (18–21°C), it will sprout a cluster of leaves at some point on the cane. Then supply average temperatures in summer, and water well while growing, sparingly during winter, MWT 40°F (4°C).

Table 1: types of houseplant
Tr. = trailing; Cl. = climbing; L = potentially large; * = easy.

Foliage plants

Adiantum
Aechmea
Agave*
Aloe*
Aphelandra
Araucaria (L)*
Asparagus densiflorus
 'Sprengeri' (Tr.)*
A. setaceus*
Aspidistra*
Asplenium
Begonia (cane – L, rex,
 species)*
Ceropegia (Tr.)*
Chamaedorea (L)
Chlorophytum (Tr.)*
Cissus (Cl., L)*
Codiaeum
Coleus* =
 Solenostemon
Cordyline
Cryptanthus*

Cyperus (L)*
Dieffenbachia
Dizygotheca = Schefflera
Dracaena
Epipremnum (Cl.)
Episcia (Tr.)
× Fatshedera (Tr., Cl.,
 L)*
Fatsia (L)*
Ficus elastica
 'Decora' (L)*
F. benjamina (L)*
F. pumila (Tr.)
D. deltoidea*
Fittonia (Tr.)
Grevillea (L)*
Hedera (Tr., Cl.
 some L)*
Hypoestes
Maranta
Monstera (Cl., L)
Nephrolepis*

Pelargonium (ivy-leaved
 – Tr., scented-leaved)*
Peperomia
Philodendron (Cl.)*
Pilea*
Platycerium*
Pteris
Sansevieria*
Saxifraga (Tr.)*
Schefflera (L)*
Sedum (Tr.)*
Senecio rowleyanus
 (Tr.)* = Pericallis
Setcreasea
 (Tr.)* = Tradescantia
Syngonium (Cl.)*
Tolmiea (Tr.)*
Tradescantia (Tr.)*
Yucca*
Zebrina
 (Tr.)* = Tradescantia

Flowering and fruiting plants

Achimenes (some Tr.)*
Aechmea*
Aphelandra
Begonia (tuberous,
 semperflorens,
 pendula – Tr.)*
Beloperone* = Justicia
Browallia (Tr.)*
Campanula (Tr.)*
Capsicum
Chrysanthemum* =
 Dendranthema
× Citrofortunella*
Cyclamen

Epiphyllum
Episcia
Euphorbia
Exacum*
Fuchsia (some Tr.)*
Hibiscus
Hippeastrum
Hoya (Cl., L)*
Impatiens*
Jasminum (Cl., L)*
Kalanchoe*
Passiflora (Cl., L)*
Pelargonium (zonal,
 regal)*

Peperomia
Primula*
Rhipsalidopsis*
Rhododendron (azalea)
Saintpaulia (some Tr.)
Saxifraga*
Schlumbergera*
Sedum*
Senecio(cineraria)*
 = Pericallis
Sinningia (gloxinia)
Solanum
Streptocarpus*
Thunbergia (Cl.)*

Table 2: houseplants for particular situations

Sun

Agave
Aloe
Beloperone = Justicia
Browallia
Campanula
Capsicum
Ceropegia
× Citrofortunella
Hibiscus
Impatiens
Jasminum
Passiflora
Pelargonium
Sansevieria
Setcreasea
    = Tradescantia
Solanum
Thunbergia

Light shade

Adiantum
Asparagus
Aspidistra
Asplenium
Begonia
Chamaedorea
Cissus

Cryptanthus
Cyclamen
Cyperus
Epipremnum
Episcia
    × Fatshedera
Fatsia
Ficus pumila
Fuchsia
Hedera (plain green
    forms)
Monstera
Nephrolepis
Philodendron
Platycerium
Pteris
Rhododendron (azalea)
Saxifraga
Syngonium (plain-
    leaved)

Deep shade

Aspidistra
Chamaedorea
Fittonia
Hedera (plain green
    forms)

Philodendron
Sansevieria
Saxifraga

**Unheated but frost-free
rooms**

Araucaria
Aspidistra
Beloperone = Justicia
Campanula
Chlorophytum
Cissus
    × Fatshedera
Fatsia
Fuchsia
Grevillea
Hedera
Jasminum
    officinale
Pelargonium
Primula
Saxifraga
Schefflera
Sedum
Streptocarpus
Tolmiea
Tradescantia

BIOLOGICAL CONTROL SUPPLIERS

Applied Horticulture, Fargro Ltd, Toddington Lane, Little-
    hampton, West Sussex BN17 7PP
English Woodlands Biocontrol, Hoyle, Graffham, Petworth, West
    Sussex GU28 0LR
Henry Doubleday Research Association, Ryton Court, Wolston
    Lane, Ryton on Dunsmore, Coventry CV8 3L
Natural Pest Control (Amateur), Watermead, Yapton Road,
    Barnham, Bognor Regis, West Sussex, PO2 0BQ
Scarletts Plantcare, West Bergholt, Colchester, CO6 3DH
WyeBugs, Biological Sciences, Wye College, Wye, Ashford, Kent
    TN25 5AH

Conservatory
Gardening

—— ALAN TOOGOOD ——

Grand conservatories like this offer plenty of ideas that can
be adapted to fit a more modest construction

Introduction

The appeal of conservatories is well-established. The warm scents of the conservatory, earthy and floral, the year-round display of colourful and often exotic plants, are a constant delight. With romantic and nostalgic associations and a unique blend of beauty and practicality, a conservatory makes a desirable extension to almost every type of house.

Today the conservatory is most often used as an extra living room, a 'garden room' well furnished with both plants and home comforts. But its use can be adapted in many ways, for example adjoining a kitchen as a dining- or breakfast-room, or linking two rooms.

Fashions come and go, and many turn full circle. Hence, as the 20th century draws to a close, conservatories are a Victorian feature, often in the Victorian style, which are enjoyed once more. The revival started in the 1970s, with many variations appearing in the boom period of the 1980s, and an increasing number of companies selling conservatories or conservatory-related products.

Many Victorians had large elaborate glass structures built on to their houses. The interior landscaping was often jungle-like with waterfalls, pools and rockwork and the latest plants to be brought back from the tropics and sub-tropics by intrepid plant collectors. Many of the plants introduced at this time proved to be hardy out of doors, but some, like camellias, benefit from the protected environment of the conservatory where their lovely flowers can be enjoyed to the full, undamaged by rain or frost. Conservatories were often used as places for entertaining guests and enjoying plants of all seasons, a function just as important to us today.

First decide on the use of your conservatory. Will plants and family have equal status, will it be a place mainly for plants, or, most likely perhaps, will the plants be there largely as a background to family life? Architectural harmony is essential. Conservatories can be designed to blend with any house style. There are the popular Victorian styles to choose from, and many others, one for every taste and every style of dwelling.

Colours do clash in nature! The pea flowers of *Chorizema ilicifolium*, a small evergreen shrub, light up the conservatory in spring and summer (see p. 105)

Choosing and Siting

A conservatory is usually a once-in-a-lifetime investment. It is essential to be absolutely certain of what you really want and need when buying or even building. Take as much care in selecting a conservatory as in choosing a house; all the aspects should be considered in detail.

SUPPLIERS

There are a large number of conservatory manufacturers, so the first step is to see as many different makes as possible. Various manufacturers have show sites or showrooms, and sometimes share a site with a garden centre. Some suppliers exhibit at major flower shows such as the Chelsea Flower Show, providing an opportunity of seeing many makes in one day.

Manufacturers supply well-illustrated and highly informative brochures or catalogues that give an excellent idea of quality and models available. They also list any show sites.

Conservatory manufacturers vary in the service they offer. At the top end are those who are able to design conservatories from scratch – as an architect designs a house. Others at the top end supply modular conservatories formed from standardised units (modules) to suit customers' requirements, a popular way to buy a conservatory.

Still others offer a range of models that cannot be modified – the customer simply chooses the most suitable design and size.

QUESTIONS

Suppliers will be able to answer all your questions regarding buying and installing a conservatory. Consult their brochures first.

You will need to know if planning permission is required and whether the structure comes under building regulations. Some manufacturers can handle this on your behalf if necessary, and

Victorian styles are popular today, especially for older houses, and modern materials like uPVC and aluminium may be used in their construction

will supply plans and other information for submission to your local authority.

However, planning permission may not be needed, as many conservatories come under permitted development, especially if they are small ground-level conservatories or are *not* sited on a wall fronting the highway. Very large structures and those to be erected on listed buildings or in conservation areas *will* require planning permission. Liaise with the planning department of your local authority when you have made a choice, but *before* you place an order.

Check that the manufacturer is a member of the Conservatory Association, which sets high standards that should be followed.

With advice, decide on a suitable base, and find out if the manufacturer is able to construct it. If not, find a local builder, having received the exact specifications from the supplier. The base involves a lot of work – usually it is a concrete slab laid over at least 4 in (10 cm) of hardcore, the concrete being a minimum of 4 in (10 cm) thick, with the edges thickened to a depth of at least 12 in (30 cm). This is covered with a damp-proof membrane, followed by a 2 in (5 cm) deep screed of mortar.

Is a brick or stone wall needed for the conservatory? Many are built on low walls, in the attractive traditional way (see p. 80).

Check who will erect the conservatory. Many are erected by the suppliers, or they may recommend an erection service. Many conservatories are not suitable for DIY erection.

Other questions you will want answered:

- How long will it take to build the base?
- How long will you have to wait for delivery of the conservatory?
- How long will it take to put it up?

STYLES

The enormous range of styles and designs may at first bewilder the newcomer. There is one simple guideline to making the right choice: choose a conservatory suited to the period and style of your house. It should appear an integral part of the dwelling house and not look as though it has been added on as an afterthought.

Victorian-style conservatories (particularly in octagonal designs) are extremely popular, and are offered by many manufacturers. Victorian, Regency and Edwardian styles have large rectangular windows. Georgian styles have windows with small panes of glass.

A modern conservatory in aluminium alloy. Lean-to designs with low-pitched roofs are also an ideal choice for bungalows

Owners of town and city houses often favour the Gothic style with a pointed arched roof and windows, or a conservatory with a curvaceous ogee arched roof.

There are many stylish modern designs for contemporary houses, with large arch-topped (in timber-framed models) or rectangular windows, as well as those with aluminium frames and attractive curved eaves. Other designs are more angular and some have a low ridge, making them suitable for erecting on bungalow walls.

Many conservatories are of lean-to shape, while others stand away from the walls and have pitched roofs. They can be octagonal, square, rectangular, hexagonal, bay ended or combinations.

An appealing and more unusual idea is to build a conservatory around a corner or corners. Another is an elevated conservatory with access from an upstairs room, which some companies will design and erect.

All of these options are there: the best advice is to shop around thoroughly until you find a conservatory that really meets your needs and expectations and suits your home.

Don't confuse lean-to greenhouses with conservatories of similar shape. A greenhouse is not designed as a living area and should only be used for growing plants. A lean-to conservatory has a stronger framework and is generally of more substantial construction than a greenhouse.

Many conservatories, especially traditional styles, are built on low base walls, such as brick, and these should ideally match the house

MATERIALS

The choice of materials used for the framework includes: timber, aluminium alloy and uPVC.

Timber

Softwoods (from coniferous trees) are often used, particularly western red cedar. Hardwoods (from deciduous broad-leaved trees), including oak and, if you must, farmed, renewable maghogany, are used by some manufacturers of high-quality conservatories. Timber can be painted or left its natural colour to match the house. Timber blends into any situation exceedingly well but does need regular painting or preservation treatment.

Aluminium alloy

This modern framework material is well suited to contemporary houses. It is also possible to buy conservatories in aluminium that match the period and style of older properties. Victorian and other styles are available.

A heavy aluminium framework is used for conservatories (as

The alternative to building a conservatory on a base wall is to have glass to the ground, resulting in good light at floor level

opposed to a light framework for lean-to greenhouses) and usually it has a decorative finish, perhaps coated with white or brown polyester paint.

Aluminium alloy is maintenance free, needing no preservation treatment. The framework of some conservatories is insulated to reduce condensation, which is inclined to occur on cold metal.

Stainless steel

This is included in the framework by some manufacturers of high-quality conservatories because it is a very strong material, therefore an excellent choice for certain large structures. Like aluminium alloy it is completely maintenance free.

uPVC

This modern material is becoming increasingly popular for the framework. It is a good insulator, will not rot or corrode and is maintenance free, needing no painting or preservation treatment. It can be supplied in a variety of colours, including white or brown, or with a woodgrain finish. Conservatories in both modern and traditional styles are now available in uPVC.

Base walls

Many conservatories, especially traditional styles, are built on low walls, varying in height from approximately 18 to 36 in (45 to 90 cm). Ideally the base walls should match the house and can be built of materials such as bricks, natural walling stone or ornamental concrete walling blocks.

The base walls may alternatively be an integral part of the conservatory, being constructed of timber or aluminium as appropriate. Some conservatories are supplied with reinforced-concrete base walls, with various decorative finishes.

The alternative to base walls is to have glass to ground level, very often used in modern designs and available in many styles and designs. A plus is more light at floor level − desirable if you intend growing plants in tubs or pots on the floor.

GLASS

Today there is a choice of traditional single glazing or modern sealed double glazing. The advantages of the latter are well known: it drastically reduces heat loss from the building, so reducing heating bills, as well as muffling outside noise. It is much more expensive than single glazing.

Note that toughened safety glass conforming to British Standards is used in conservatories: do not settle for anything less.

However, the roofs of many conservatories are 'glazed' with twin-skin or triple-skin polycarbonate, which is shatterproof and a perfectly acceptable roofing material. Other conservatories have glass roofs. The choice is yours.

Yet another option with some manufacturers is glass treated with a transparent coating that protects the surface from the elements and keeps it looking good and easy to clean.

Always keep glass clean to ensure maximum light.

DOORS AND WINDOWS

Central double doors are popular, traditionally hung in period styles, or of the sliding patio type in modern aluminium conservatories. Positions and numbers of doors can usually be varied to suit you. One can also have single doors.

Security is a very important point that you must clarify with the manufacturer. Doors should be fitted with high-security locks, including the internal door that provides access between house and conservatory.

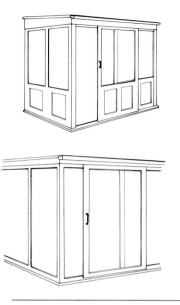

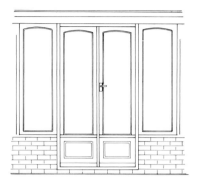

Figure 1: Modern conservatories may have sliding patio doors. Double central doors, traditionally hung, are often used in period styles

Many conservatories have opening windows in the sides. The more the better, as they can be used to prevent a temperature build-up during warm or hot weather. Ventilators in the roof are also essential to ensure a through-flow of air. Often one has the option of additional roof ventilators – again the more the better.

Remember that windows and ventilators must also be fitted with locks to deter burglars: it is useless having high-security door locks if acess can be gained through windows.

Door and window fittings vary in quality but should match the quality of the building. Brass fittings are often popular in the more expensive models.

A TOUCH OF STYLE

The more expensive conservatories, especially those in traditional styles, may be decorated with ridge cresting, dentil mouldings and finials in the appropriate designs. They may be made of wood, cast aluminium or fibreglass and provide a finishing touch to the outside.

SITE

A conservatory should obviously be erected on the best possible site. A very sunny position is preferable, but not essential, as success can be achieved in shade. Many plants enjoy or tolerate shade.

A conservatory is normally built against an outside wall, with access from one of the rooms of the house. This is not essential: if there is no suitable wall, it could be built against a garden wall, either a boundary or internal wall. As mentioned earlier, a conservatory can be elevated if desired, built on stilts or pillars, with access from a first-floor room.

Other points to note:

- Avoid covering an existing attractive feature of the house, if possible.
- Ensure that, from a technical point of view, a door can be created in the house wall.
- Building over a services inspection cover involves more complex base construction, and is best avoided, if possible.

Fit wire guards to the eaves of the house roof immediately above a conservatory to protect the conservatory roof from falling tiles.

The site does not necessarily have to be level. This can be adjusted during construction of the base. A base can be built on a sloping site but, of course, you will have to be prepared for much more construction work.

CONSIDERING THE ASPECT

If you do have a choice, site the conservatory in the sunniest spot available. A wall that faces south is ideal. Almost as desirable is a west-facing wall.

A conservatory sited on a shady or partially shady wall (one facing north or east), will be more expensive to heat, as the sun will not be much help. The 'atmosphere' will be different, too: a shady conservatory will not be quite so cheerful as one that receives plenty of sun. A bonus is that you are less likely to have to solve the problem of keeping the sun *out* to reduce temperatures.

It is highly desirable to site a conservatory where it is sheltered from cold winds. Wind results in rapid heat loss from a conservatory, particularly one with single glazing, which means it will be more costly to heat. If you really cannot avoid a windy site then at least opt for double glazing.

One of the worst sites is between two houses, as wind funnelling can occur, especially if they are quite close together.

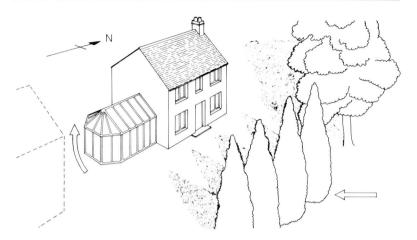

Figure 2: Siting. A conservatory must not be subjected to wind or shade. Space between houses can be a wind tunnel. Windbreaks filter the wind

It may be possible to create a windbreak on the windward side of the site. A natural living windbreak, such as a row of conifers, is best if you have the space. Suitable subjects include the very fast-growing ×*Cupressocyparis leylandii* (Leyland cypress) with grey-green foliage, or bronze-yellow in the slightly slower-growing cultivar 'Castlewellan'; *Chamaecyparis lawsoniana* (Lawson cypress), choosing strong-growing cultivars like rich green 'Green Hedger' or golden-yellow 'Lane'; or *Thuja plicata* (western red cedar) with shiny, deep green, aromatic foliage.

Keep the windbreak well away from the conservatory so that it does not cast a shadow over the building. Remember that a living windbreak will take a lot of moisture from the soil, and you really need a large garden for this idea to work well. One can put up an artificial windbreak, using windbreak netting, but this is unsightly, to say the least, and not recommended unless you can find a way of disguising it, say with climbers.

Avoid a site that is overhung with large trees as these will create a lot of shade and result in an accumulation of leaves on the conservatory roof and in the gutters. Rain will wash dirt and dust from the leaves of the trees and this could create grime on the glass. There is also the risk of falling branches damaging the conservatory.

A conservatory that is chosen in keeping with the house and sited with the above points in mind, will become visually harmonious very quickly.

Fixtures and Fittings

One of the most exciting stages of building a conservatory is fitting out the inside and turning it into a 'garden room' for use as an extra living room and as a place for plants. Features such as a suitable floor covering, furniture and blinds should be chosen to meet your requirements and to give the room its 'personality'. You must ensure adequate heating. As in any other room of the house, lighting and power points will be required. The electricity supply should be installed by a qualified electrician.

HEATING

Before choosing a heating system carefully consider the temperature you intend to maintain. If it is to be used as a living area, then maintaining a steady temperature of between 60° and 70°F (15.5° and 21°C) would be acceptable for most people. This is classed as a warm conservatory, which also makes an ideal home for many tropical and sub-tropical plants.

With a minimum winter night temperature of 50°F (10°C) you would have an intermediate conservatory, which also suits a wide range of plants.

The cool conservatory has a minimum winter night temperature of 40° to 45°F (4.5° to 7°C). This too will be suitable for a wide range of tender plants.

Intermediate and cool conservatories are, of course, rather chilly when maintained at the minimum temperatures, but remember they will often be warmer than this as the sun will raise the temperature.

The best idea, especially for a conservatory that is to be regularly used as a living area, is to run the central-heating system into it and install radiators, if this is possible. This is also the most economical means of heating the structure. However, plants need consistent warmth, so if your heating is turned off at night, you will need a secondary heating system, independently controlled.

Floor covering and blinds create the 'look' you want. Tiles are a sensible choice for both plants and people

Independent systems

It may not be possible to run the central-heating system into a conservatory, in which case one of the independent heating systems must be chosen.

Electric heating is highly recommended as it is efficient, clean, reliable, very convenient and automatically controlled. Make sure an electric heater has thermostatic control for economical running.

There are various types of portable electric heater that can be used in a conservatory, such as convection heaters and fan heaters. Alternatively you might like to consider storage heaters that run at night on cheap electricity.

If the conservatory is to be used primarily for growing plants and there is likely to be a lot of water splashed about, then it is highly recommended that an electric greenhouse heater is used. Again this may be a portable fan heater, or banks of tubular heaters mounted on the walls.

Gas and paraffin heaters are not ideal for conservatories that are also used as living areas, as they give off water vapour and this can result in a lot of condensation forming on the glass and framework, unless some ventilation is provided all the time the heater is in use. However, gas (natural or bottled) and paraffin heaters are suitable for plant conservatories, most of the latter being capable only of keeping a conservatory frost free.

Blinds, such as these attractive internal louvre side blinds, can be tailor-made and are supplied by many conservatory manufacturers

Obviously gas and paraffin heaters need more attention than electric heaters. Remember that paraffin heaters require more maintenance than any, and must be regularly cleaned, especially the wick, if they are not to give off fumes that are harmful to plants. Blue-flame paraffin heaters are recommended, used with high-grade paraffin.

Output of heaters
A heater must be capable of producing sufficient heat (its heat output) to maintain the minimum temperature required when the outside temperature is very low. Ideally it should have a higher output than needed to ensure it maintains the minimum temperature in periods of exceptionally severe weather.

A heater manufacturer or supplier should be able to advise on size of heater, given the size of your conservatory and the minimum temperature to be maintained.

FLOOR COVERINGS

The concrete screed will need covering, materials depending on how the conservatory is to be used. In the plant conservatory, the base could simply be sealed with a cement sealant. Or you could lay pre-cast non-slip concrete paving slabs for a more decorative finish.

For the conservatory that is to be used as a living room, a decorative floor covering will be required. There are tiles to choose from, including terracotta, quarry and slate. They are cool underfoot, but terracotta and quarry tiles helpfully come in 'warm' colours. Slate tiles are mainly grey, although some imported kinds come in shades of brown.

Non-slip ceramic tiles come in many designs and colours, so are ideal for creating a co-ordinated colour scheme. The same applies to vinyl floor tiles.

Cork tiles give a warm feeling underfoot and this natural product looks appropriate in a 'garden room'. Another natural material is woven seagrass floor covering with a latex backing.

If you prefer carpeting, then hardwearing cord is a good choice.

FURNITURE

As with floor coverings, choosing furniture such as tables and chairs is very personal. Some styles look more at ease in a garden room than others.

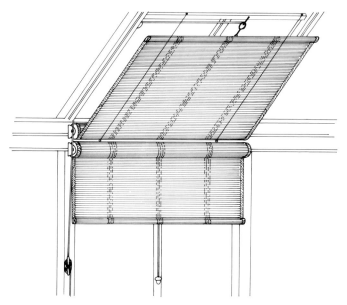

Figure 3: Traditional internal roller blinds can be tailored to fit the roof and sides of a conservatory and are made from various materials

If you like woven furniture, there is a choice of willow, rattan (a tropical climbing palm) and cane. Such furniture looks particularly good in traditional-style conservatories, as does wrought-iron furniture, or reproductions in cast aluminium.

For the modern conservatory, there is a big choice of wooden and tubular aluminium garden furniture, the latter often being plastic coated and well upholstered for comfort.

BLINDS

Note that, unless the conservatory is in a shady position, blinds are essential to shut out hot sun and thereby help to lower the temperature. Many people do not realise that the temperature inside a conservatory can become unbearably high when the sun is shining and blinds have not been fitted.

Blinds can be tailor-made and are supplied by many conservatory manufacturers. If possible, buy the blinds from the manufacturer of your conservatory. Most conservatory blinds are designed for internal use. Depending on the materials and systems, they are often available in a range of colours, so can be chosen to match the decor.

Traditional roller blinds come in various materials such as cotton and polyester fabric, fabric blinds metallised on the outside to reflect heat and glare, and glass-fibre fabric.

Alternatively there are louvered side blinds and retractable slatted or pleated roof blinds. Some come in polyester material. Another option is Venetian blinds, either manually or electrically operated.

Then there are the non-retractable louvre roof blinds in aluminium or cedar. The louvres open and close and can be operated electrically, manually or by various other control options. Versions exist for both internal and external use.

AUTOMATIC VENTILATION

Automatic ventilator openers, powered by natural heat, are highly recommended for roof ventilators. They can be pre-set to open at a required temperature and they close the vents again when the temperature drops.

Opening the side windows, doors and roof ventilators results in air movement or ventilation, but additional movement can be created with electric fans, such as extractor fans that remove stale air, or circulating fans that simply keep the air moving. Such fans are installed in or near the roof and are particularly useful during warm or hot still weather.

Now you are ready to consider in more detail the plants themselves. The variety and beauty of the plants you choose will create a living, always changing, picture within your home.

Figure 4: Roof ventilators can be opened and closed automatically by means of ventilator openers powered by natural heat

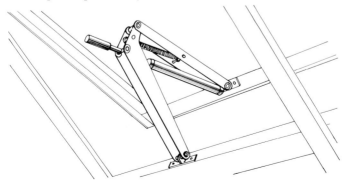

Preparing for Plants

To quote the original meaning, a conservatory is a structure in which tender plants are 'conserved' in cold weather. The writer John Evelyn first used the word in 1664. By the late 18th century the meaning had changed to a structure in which to display tender plants attractively and enjoy them. This is just as applicable today, when conservatories also provide extra living space, so we must devise various means of displaying them well.

DISPLAY STAGING

If you want to grow lots of small plants in pots, such as flowering and foliage pot plants, seasonal bulbs, and the like, you will need some staging to display them, unless you prefer to group plants on the floor.

Ideally the staging should match the conservatory: choose aluminium-framed staging for an aluminium-framed conservatory, or wooden staging for a timber structure.

Bench-type staging should be roughly at waist height and is usually placed against a side of the conservatory.

Tiered staging, with different levels, is more suitable for a conservatory, though. The tiers can be placed against the back wall, making good use of vertical space. Impressive and professional-looking plant displays can be created on this and trailing plants displayed to advantage.

One often has a choice of staging surface:

- Slatted allows good air circulation between plants, and heat can rise up through the slats.
- Gravel trays can be filled with horticultural aggregate which, if kept moist, will create humidity around plants.
- Water matting can be laid in the trays to provide capillary irrigation.

Aluminium staging is usually designed on a modular basis so that sections are easily added or removed.

Nerium oleander, an evergreen shrub flowering in summer and autumn, is available in various colours and ideal for large-pot or tub culture (see p. 101)

Displaying temporary cool-conservatory plants like primulas, cinerarias, calceolarias and petunias in a group creates impact

Ornamental plant stands

Ornamental plant stands are alternatives, or additional to staging. The stepped designs are most useful in conservatories. Usually made of aluminium, they are especially suited to modern styles of conservatory.

SHELVING

While tiered staging helps to make the most of vertical space, shelving can take plants even higher. It might be useful on the back wall, for instance, for displaying trailing and cascading plants.

Shelving, including hanging types, can also be fitted in the roof area, if desired. Special greenhouse shelving is available and units consisting of a number of shelves, one above the other, are probably the most useful for display work.

RAISED BEDS

There is no doubt that permanent plants like shrubs, perennials and climbers grow very much better in soil beds as they have more root space. As the conservatory floor is concrete, it is most convenient to construct raised beds.

Beds can be built around the edge of a conservatory and, if space permits, in the middle. The shape is up to the individual – formal or informal. Importantly, avoid building against the walls of a conservatory as this will cause problems from damp penetration; so leave a gap.

Regarding building materials, aim either for a rustic look by choosing logs or natural stone, dry laid, or a more formal appearance with building bricks or ornamental concrete walling blocks.

To give plants a reasonable depth of soil and to prevent rapid drying out, build beds about 18 in (45 cm) in height. Remember to leave some drainage holes in the sides, at the base, if you are building with bricks or blocks.

Some rubble or shingle can be placed in the bottom and covered with rough leafmould to ensure good drainage, then the beds filled with good-quality light to medium topsoil.

After planting, mulch the beds with pulverised bark or, for a collection of cacti and succulents, with pea shingle or stone chippings.

The conservatory floor should be covered with concrete paving slabs, or terracotta, quarry, slate, or ceramic tiles, as drainage from the beds could make it damp at times. Alternatively, seal the cement screed. When watering, always be careful not to apply so much that it gushes out from the beds and floods the floor.

Figure 5: Raised beds will have a rustic look if built from logs or natural stone. A terraced bed gives greater scope for imaginative planting

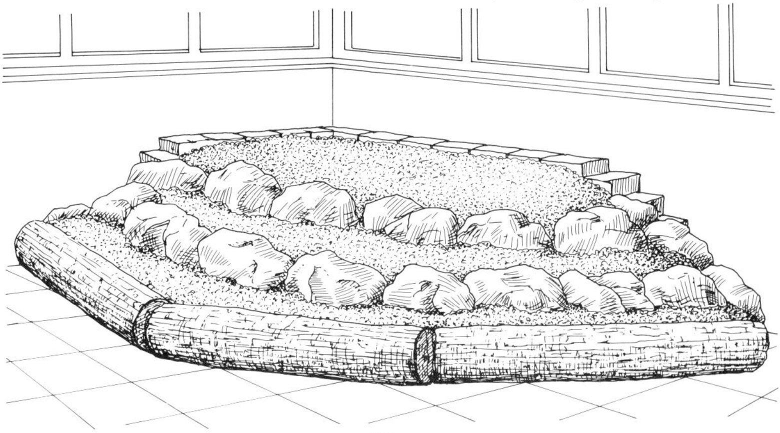

Alternative to raised beds

A simpler alternative to raised beds is large ready-made planters that come in various materials (the most common being plastic), sizes and shapes: the sort of thing that you see in hotel reception areas, restaurants and the like, containing impressive plant displays. These are watertight so there will be no problems from drainage. Group several together for a large planting area.

Another idea: instead of planting direct in planters, fill them with a peat substitute like coconut fibre, or a horticultural aggregate, and plunge the pots to their rims. This makes for easy re-arranging of planting schemes.

SUPPORTS FOR CLIMBERS

The back wall of a conservatory offers an ideal location for climbing plants, but they will require additional means of support. Most simple is a system of horizontal galvanised or plastic-coated wires spaced 8-12 in (20-30 cm) apart. They can even be taken into the roof area. Wires can be secured with metal vine eyes screwed into the wall or timber framework. There are special plugs available for fixing wires to metal conservatory framework. All of these hold the wires an inch or two from the wall.

Alternatively fix trellis panels to the wall. There is a choice of wooden, plastic-coated steel or plastic trellis and panels come in various shapes and sizes. Fix them 1-2 in (2.5-5 cm) from the wall, using suitable brackets.

Moss poles

This attractive means of supporting climbing plants that produce aerial roots, like many of the philodendrons, can be inserted in pots, tubs or soil beds. Easily made, moss poles consist of a suitable length of broom handle or similar, enclosed in a cylinder of small-mesh wire netting which is filled with live sphagnum moss. A small pot, inserted to its rim in the top, allows for easy moistening of the moss (which should be kept damp at all times) – simply fill it with water.

Wire-netting cylinders

Wire-netting cylinders of various diameters, supported inside with wooden stakes or canes, make excellent supports for ivies, which will eventually completely cover these supports.

Tropical foliage plants contrast dramatically in shape and texture in this warm-conservatory group, pleasing at any time of year

ELEVATED CONTAINERS

Many plants, especially trailing kinds, are effectively grown in elevated containers like hanging baskets. Choose the moulded-plastic type of basket with built-in drip tray.

Half baskets and wall pots, that are fixed directly to walls, are also ideal for trailers.

POTS, TUBS AND PLANTERS

There are many attractive containers for permanent conservatory plants, like terracotta pots and tubs, and concrete, reconstituted-stone and plastic tubs, in many sizes and styles. Up-market containers for conservatory plants, especially trees and shrubs, are square wooden Versailles-type tubs.

Then there are the self-watering tubs and planters, especially useful over periods when one is away from home.

If you wish to grow plants in normal flower pots, then consider placing them in ornamental pot holders, filling the space between the two with moist peat substitute or horticultural aggregate.

95

Choosing Plants

Plants are chosen to suit the minimum temperature of the conservatory. For the three temperature regimes refer to Heating, under Fixtures and Fittings (p. 85).

The following is a very select list of plants suitable for growing in conservatories – there are many more excellent kinds available but lack of space prevents them being included here.

COOL CONSERVATORY

Permanent plants

Anigozanthos (kangaroo paw) Perennials that produce racemes of woolly tubular flowers in spring and summer from fans of sword-shaped leaves. *A. flavidus* (see p. 99) has yellow-green flowers.

Suitable for pot culture, using well-drained acid peaty compost. Needs good bright light and sun, normal watering in summer, much less in winter. Liquid feed fortnightly in summer.

Bauhinia Evergreen, semi-evergreen or deciduous shrubs and trees that are grown for their flowers. Of the several species, *B. punctata* (syn. *B. galpinii*) can be recommended, an evergreen or semi-evergreen shrub to 10 ft (3 m) in height with bright red scented flowers during summer.

Grow in a pot or tub of well drained soil-based compost, or in a soil bed. Provide maximum light, water freely in the growing period, sparingly in winter, liquid feed fortnightly in summer, and thin out congested growth after flowering.

Camellia Evergreen shrubs with deep green shiny foliage and winter or spring flowers in shades of red, pink or white. Cultivars of *C. japonica, C. × williamsii* and *C. reticulata* are recommended. Also, scented cultivars are particularly noticeable under glass.

Grow in pots or tubs with ericaceous (acid) compost. Stand plants outside when flowering is over, choosing a partially shady and sheltered site, and re-house in autumn. Compost should be

Clianthus puniceus, above, is an ideal climber for the small conservatory as it grows only 1.8 m (6 ft) high; this is the variety *albus*. *Clivia miniata*, below, is an evergreen perennial which flowers best in spring and summer – if left undisturbed once planted or potted (see p. 98)

97

kept moist throughout the year. Liquid feed fortnightly in summer. Provide plenty of ventilation.

Clianthus (parrot's bill) The species *C. puniceus* is normally grown, a 6 ft (2 m) high evergreen climber with pinnate leaves and, in spring and summer, clusters of bill-like red flowers.

Grow in a soil bed, or large pot of soil-based potting compost. Water sparingly in winter and liquid feed fortnightly in summer. Maximum light is needed, but shade from strong sun. Prune out growing tips in spring.

Clivia (kaffir lily) The evergreen perennial *C. miniata* (see p.28) has long strap-shaped leaves and during spring or summer produces heads of funnel-shaped orange flowers.

Ideally grow in a soil bed; alternatively in a pot of soil-based compost. Do not disturb once planted. Summer watering as necessary but in winter allow compost to almost dry out between waterings. Provide humidity in warm weather and shade from strong sun. Liquid feed fortnightly in summer.

Coprosma There are numerous species and cultivars of these evergreen shrubs and trees. Particularly attractive is *C.* × *kirkii* 'Variegata', a small dense shrub with white-edged leaves.

Ideal for pot culture, using well drained soil-based compost. Ensure maximum light, water freely in summer, sparingly during winter, and liquid feed fortnightly in summer.

Epacris Evergreen heath-like shrubs grown for their attractive tubular flowers produced in winter or spring. *E. impressa* (Australian heath) has pink or red flowers.

Grow in pots of well-drained acid compost high in humus. Provide sunny, airy conditions. Water moderately during growing season, very sparingly at other times. Flowered shoots can be cut back after flowering.

Hoya (wax flower) One of the most popular conservatory climbers is *H. carnosa* (see p. 100), an evergreen to a height of 15 ft (4.5 m), but slow growing, producing white waxy flowers in pendulous clusters during summer, turning pink as they mature.

Grow in a soil bed ideally; alternatively in a pot or tub. Soil or compost should be rich in humus. In summer, humidity and shade from hot sun are appreciated, together with fortnightly liquid feeding. Water as needed in summer but in winter the growing medium should be allowed to almost dry out between waterings. Do not prune plants as they resent it.

Jasminum (jasmine) For fragrance there are few conservatory plants to beat jasmine. Try the white summer-flowering *J. polyanthum* and yellow-flowered *J. mesnyi* which blooms in

Anigozanthos, including the yellow-green *A. flavidus* (see p. 97), are easily
grown perennials flowering in spring and summer, provided the light is good

spring. Both these climbers are evergreen, reaching a height of at
least 10 ft (3 m).

Ideal for beds, or pots/tubs of soil-based compost. Shade from
strong sun and ensure plenty of ventilation. Water as needed all
year round and liquid feed fortnightly in summer. To prune, thin
out older wood in late winter and slightly reduce height.

Lantana The small evergreen shrub *L. camara* seems always to be
in flower, producing rounded heads of yellow blooms which turn
red as they age; or pink, red or white in its cultivars.

It will be more vigorous in a bed than if grown in a pot/tub of
soil-based compost. Plenty of sun is needed together with airy
conditions. In winter maintain the soil/compost only slightly
moist. Liquid feed in summer. Prune by cutting back plants in

early spring, to within 6 in (15 cm) of their base. Renew plants regularly from spring or summer cuttings.

Lapageria (Chilean bellflower) The most popular conservatory climber is *L. rosea*. Growing to about 10 ft (3 m) in height, this distinctive evergreen produces sumptuous crimson waxy bell-shaped flowers during late summer and autumn.

It should be grown in acid humus-rich soil or compost, in a bed or large pot. Provide light shade from strong sun, airy conditions, water as needed all year round and liquid feed fortnightly in summer. Do not prune.

Metrosideros Evergreen shrubs and trees whose flowers, produced in winter, have numerous showy stamens. *M. excelsa* (rata, New Zealand Christmas tree), is a tree with shiny deep green leaves, white felted below, and flowers with crimson stamens.

Can be grown in a large pot or tub of well drained soil-based compost, or in a soil bed. Ensure maximum light, and water freely

Hoya carnosa is one of the most popular climbers for small conservatories, but a slow grower, producing waxy flowers with a heady scent during the summer (see p. 98)

during the growing period (when fortnightly feeding can be carried out) but moderately at other times.

Nerium (oleander) The evergreen shrub *N. oleander* (see p. 90) flowers profusely in summer and autumn, bearing clusters of purple-red, red, pink or white blooms, double in some cultivars.

Best grown in large pots or tubs as it relishes a spell out of doors during the summer. Grow in soil-based compost. Can also be grown in beds. Needs plenty of sun and airy conditions. Water as needed in summer; but, during winter allow soil/compost to partially dry out between waterings. Liquid feed fortnightly in summer.

Strelitzia (bird of paradise flower) *S. reginae* (see p. 128) is an evergreen perennial with large banana-like leaves. Older established plants (at least five to seven years) produce a succession of striking orange and blue flowers in summer, in shape like a bird's head.

Grow in a soil bed or large pot/tub of soil-based compost. Likes plenty of sun and airy conditions. Water as needed in summer, but keep only slightly moist during winter. Liquid feed fortnightly in summer.

Temporary plants

These plants are flowered only once in the conservatory. When the display is over, either discard or plant in the garden, depending on type.

Calceolaria (slipper wort) Calceolaria hybrids are generally grown as biennial pot plants and are discarded after flowering. They produce colourful pouched flowers in shades of yellow, red and orange, often strikingly spotted, during spring or summer.

Seeds are sown during early summer and should not be covered with compost. Germinate in cool conditions, such as a garden frame. Prick off seedlings into trays and then pot into 3 in (8 cm) pots. Grow the plants on in the frame in airy conditions, shade from strong sun, and transfer to the conservatory in autumn, when they can be potted into 5 in (13 cm) pots. Pot into final 6 in (15 cm) pots in late winter. Soilless potting compost makes a good growing medium. Keep plants in cool and airy conditions at all times, shade from strong sun, and maintain the compost steadily moist but not wet.

Calomeria (Humea) The species *C. amaranthoides* (*H. elegans*) (incense plant) is grown as a biennial. It has an upright habit, to a height of 6 ft (1.8 m), and smells strongly of incense. The leaves are lance shaped and in summer and autumn the plant bears large heads of small pink or red flowers.

Sow seeds during mid-summer, and grow plants in pots of rich, well drained soil-based compost. Ensure sunny, airy conditions. Water freely during growing season, sparingly in winter but avoid wilting point, or wetting the foliage at any time. Liquid feed fortnightly in summer.

Chrysanthemum There are numerous types of chrysanthemum for flowering under glass, but the charm chrysanths make a marvellous show in the cool conservatory for very little effort on the part of the gardener. They are bushy plants about 18 in (45 cm) in height and in autumn are completely covered with small single flowers in a wide range of colours.

The charms are easily raised from seeds sown in mid-winter and germinated in a temperature of 50°F (10°C). Allow to grow naturally, apart from removing the growing tip when plants are 3-4 in (8-10 cm) high.

Pot initially into 3 in (8 cm) pots, then pot on until plants are in final 8 in (20 cm) pots. Use soil-based potting compost at all stages.

From early spring grow the young plants in a garden frame, then from early summer grow them outdoors. Transfer to the conservatory in early autumn. Water and feed well in summer. Under glass, the plants like airy conditions and a dry atmosphere. Discard after flowering.

Eustoma Poppy-flowered annuals and perennials. The annual *E. grandiflorum* (syn. *Lisianthus russellianus*) has pink, purple, blue or white flowers during summer.

Makes an excellent pot plant. Sow seeds during late winter at 70°F (21°C) and grow in well-drained compost. Water normally during summer. Needs maximum light, including some sun, and airy conditions. Needs long growing season. Can also be sown in autumn.

Lilium (lily) Lilies are ideal bulbs for flowering in pots under glass, after which they should be planted in the garden. There are many suitable kinds such as the yellow and white *L. auratum*; *L. longiflorum*, the Easter lily with pure white blooms; the flamboyant white and pink *L. regale*; and the equally beautiful carmine and pink *L. speciosum* var. *rubrum*.

Bulbs are potted in autumn, setting three per 8 in (20 cm) pot and using soil-based potting compost. Plant shallowly in pots half filled with compost; more compost is added as the stems grow. The pots are best kept in a garden frame over winter and transferred to the conservatory during early or mid-spring. Good ventilation is needed together with steadily moist compost. After flowering return to the frame, keep moist at all times and plant in the garden during autumn.

Oxypetalum The usual species grown is *O. caeruleum* (syn. *Tweedia caerulea*), a herbaceous climber with a twining habit, and clusters of small starry light blue flowers during summer and early autumn. Height 3 ft (1 m).

Grow as an annual in pots, sowing seeds in spring. It likes sunny well-ventilated conditions and well-drained compost. Pinch out shoot tips for a more bushy habit.

Pelargonium, regal Regal pelargoniums make a stunning display in the summer, the flowers coming in shades of red, pink, mauve, purple and white. Plants are best discarded after flowering and replaced with new ones raised from cuttings.

Cuttings can be taken in late summer when they will root without artificial heat. Pot rooted cuttings into 3½ in (9 cm) pots and in early spring move on to 5 in (13 cm) pots. Use soil-based or soilless potting compost.

Regal pelargoniums like sunny conditions (but shade from strong sun), and a dry airy atmosphere. Water as required in summer, but in winter, when conditions are cool, keep the compost only barely moist. Liquid feed flowering plants fortnightly in summer..

Primula Cultivars of *P. obconica*, with red, pink, orange, blue, lilac or white flowers, *P. malacoides* in shades of red, pink, mauve, lilac and white, and the yellow-flowered *P. × kewensis*, herald spring in the cool conservatory.

These primulas are easily raised from seeds and are discarded after flowering. Sow in the spring and germinate in a temperature of 60°F (15.5°C). Prick out seedlings into trays, then move into 3½ in (9 cm) pots, and eventually into final 5 in (13 cm) pots. A soilless compost is recommended.

Primulas should be kept cool, moist (but avoid wetting the leaves), shaded from strong sun and in airy conditions throughout their lives. From early summer to early autumn keep them in a garden frame.

Senecio (cineraria) The heads of daisy-like flowers of the late-winter and spring-flowering cinerarias (*Senecio × hybridus*) come in many colours including red, pink, blue, purple and white.

Plants are easily raised from seeds and are discarded after flowering. Sow between mid-spring and early summer and germinate in a garden frame or other cool place. Otherwise as for primulas, above, avoiding wetting the foliage and taking care not to allow the compost to become very wet.

INTERMEDIATE CONSERVATORY

Permanent plants

Banksia Evergreen shrubs and trees with attractive flowers and/or foliage. The species *B. coccinea* is an attractive shrub about 5 ft (1.5 m) high whose conical bright red flower heads, produced in winter and spring, have conspicuous styles and stigmas.

Grow in pots/tubs of acid well drained soil-based compost, or in a lime-free soil bed. Needs maximum light, sun, and very airy conditions. Moderate watering in growing period, more sparing at other times. Fortnightly liquid feeding during growing period.

Bougainvillea (paper flower) One of the most popular conservatory climbers. Mainly evergreen, the flamboyant summer colour comes from papery bracts that surround the insignificant flowers. Various kinds are grown including *B.* × *buttiana* cultivars 'Mrs Butt' (crimson-magenta), 'Golden Glow' (orange-yellow) and 'Scarlet Queen'; *B.* 'Dania' (deep pink); *B. glabra* (purple); *B.* 'Miss Manilla' (pink); and *B. spectabilis* (red-purple). Height is variable, but in the region of 15 ft (5 m).

Grow in a soil bed, or in large pots/tubs of soil-based compost. Water as required in summer but in winter only as the soil is drying out. Plenty of sunshine required, plus airy conditions and, in summer, humidity. Prune in early spring: if necessary, cut back all stems by one-third; remove any thin or weak shoots completely.

Bromeliads These flamboyant, often colourful and bizarre, relations of the pineapple are ideal conservatory plants, bringing a touch of the tropical rain forest. They are easy to grow, though, and do not need high temperatures. There are lots to choose from, including the air plants or atmospheric tillandsias that are grown on wood, such as a 'plant tree.' Other epiphytes can be grown in the same way, or in pots, including the popular kinds like *Vriesea splendens* (flaming sword), *Aechmea fasciata* (urn plant) and *Nidularium fulgens* (see p. 121).

For pot culture, grow in soilless compost, using the smallest possible pots. Keep moist all year round and ensure high humidity when conditions are warm. Air plants are watered by mist spraying daily, or weekly in cool conditions. Ensure good light, but shade from hot sun; and provide airy conditions. Those plants that form their leaves into water-holding vases, or urns, should these have permanently filled with water, which must be replaced regularly to keep it fresh. Use rain water or soft tap water for bromeliads.

Brunfelsia Evergreen shrubs with a long succession of mainly blue flowers in summer. The species normally grown is

Calliandra haematocephala, a medium-sized evergreen shrub whose pincushion flowers are produced between autumn and spring

B. pauciflora whose blue-purple flowers are fragrant. There are several desirable cultivars, and also worth growing is the wavy white *B. undulata.*

Grow in a soil bed, or in a large pot/tub of soil-based compost. Water when needed in summer, less in winter; liquid feed fortnightly in summer; and provide shade from strong sunshine.

Calliandra Evergreen trees, shrubs and climbers, the species *C. haematocephala* being grown for its pink or white pincushion-like flower heads which consist of many stamens. This autumn to spring flowering shrub reaches 10 ft (3 m) in height.

Grow in large pot or tub of well drained soil-based compost or in a soil bed. Ensure maximum light. Water freely in summer, sparingly in winter, and liquid feed fortnightly during growing season. Stems can be reduced by up to two-thirds to control height.

Chorizema Evergreen shrubs, sub-shrubs and climbers cultivated for flowers. *C. ilicifolium* (holly flame pea) (see p. 72) is a small spiny-leaved shrub with colourful orange and pink pea flowers in spring and summer.

Grow in pot or bed of neutral to acid well-drained sandy compost/soil rich in humus. Ensure maximum light, and good ventilation. Water moderately during growing season and sparingly at other times. Feed fortnightly in summer.

Citrus (oranges, lemons) These are superb shrubs or trees for growing in tubs. Even if the temperature is not high enough for fruiting, they make handsome evergreen foliage plants. The flowers are highly fragrant and produced in spring or summer. Typical species available include *C. aurantium* (Seville orange) (see p. 124), *C. sinensis* (sweet orange) and *C. limon* (lemon).

Best grown in large pots or tubs of soil-based compost. Water as needed in summer, keep only slightly moist in winter. Liquid feed fortnightly during summer, and when the weather is warm spray the foliage with water. Shade lightly from strong sun and ensure airy conditions. Plants may be stood out of doors for the summer. Maintain shape by shortening shoots by up to two-thirds every two or three years in early spring.

Ferns They are a cool green foil for colourful flowering plants. Plenty are suited to the intermediate conservatory including the very popular *Nephrolepis exaltata* (sword fern) which, incidentally, also looks good in hanging baskets; *Asplenium bulbiferum* (spleenwort); *Pteris tremula* (table fern); and *Adiantum raddianum* (delta maidenhair).

Grow in pots of soilless compost. Ferns should be shaded from direct sun and kept moist throughout the year. When conditions are warm provide humidity and an airy atmosphere. Liquid feed fortnightly during summer.

Hardenbergia Evergreen climbers and sub-shrubs with pea-like flowers. *H. violacea* (syn. *H. monophylla*) (coral pea, Australian sarsparilla) is a 10 ft (3 m) high twining climber with violet, pink or white flowers in spring.

Grow in a pot/tub of soil-based compost, or in a neutral to acid soil bed. Ensure maximum light, water freely in summer, sparingly in winter, and liquid feed fortnightly in summer.

Hibiscus (shrubby mallow) The most popular hibiscus is *H. rosa-sinensis* – or rather its cultivars, with flaring trumpet-shaped flowers in shades of red, pink, yellow, orange and white. It is a deciduous shrub bringing an exotic touch to the conservatory.

Grow in a soil bed, or in a large pot/tub of soil-based compost. Shade lightly from strong sun and provide humidity in warm conditions. Water when necessary in summer but sparingly during winter, liquid feed fortnightly in summer. If desired, prune fairly hard back in late winter.

Impatiens There are several species, but a very striking, unusual, yet easily grown one is *I. niamniamensis*. This bushy evergreen perennial produces masses of helmet-shaped red and yellow flowers in summer and autumn.

Grow in a pot of soilless compost and keep well watered in the growing season, more sparingly at other times. Liquid feed fortnightly in summer and provide humidity. Provide good light, shading from strong sun. Suitable for a shady conservatory.

Pentas Evergreen perennials and shrubs cultivated for flowers. *P. lanceolata* (syn. *P. carnea*) (Egyptian star, star-cluster), is a small shrub with heads of small pink, red, lilac or white star-shaped flowers in summer and autumn.

Grow in a pot/tub of rich, well-drained soil-based compost, or in a soil bed. Maximum light or partial shade are suitable. Water well in summer, sparingly in winter, and liquid feed fortnightly during summer. Can be hard pruned in winter.

Palms Beloved of the Victorians, palms are enjoying renewed popularity. The taller kinds make good focal points, including the feathery *Howeia forsteriana* (thatch-leaf palm) and the prickly, stiff-fronded *Phoenix canariensis* (Canary Island date palm).

Grow in a large pot or tub of soil-based compost. Water as required during summer but in winter only when the soil is drying out. Liquid feed fortnightly in summer. Ensure good light, but shade from strong sunshine.

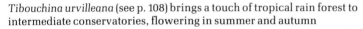

Tibouchina urvilleana (see p. 108) brings a touch of tropical rain forest to intermediate conservatories, flowering in summer and autumn

Plumbago (Cape leadwort) An excellent evergreen climber for the smaller conservatory is *P. auriculata* with beautiful sky-blue flowers in summer and autumn, or white in *P. a.* 'Alba'. Height about 10 ft (3 m).

Grow in a soil bed, or large pot/tub of soil-based compost. Water as needed in summer, but in winter keep only slightly moist. Liquid feed fortnightly in summer. Provide light shade from strong sun. Prune in late winter by reducing side shoots to a few centimetres and cutting back main stems by one-third.

Tibouchina (glory bush) The evergreen shrub *T. urvilleana* (see p. 107) produces bowl-shaped blooms of deep violet during the summer and autumn, set against sumptuous velvety foliage. This plant really does create a tropical rain-forest atmosphere.

Grow in a soil bed, or in a large pot/tub of soil-based compost. In summer water as required, but in winter keep the plant only slightly moist. Liquid feed fortnightly in summer. The plant appreciates light shade. Plants can be kept small by cutting them back in winter. It can also be trained on the back wall.

Zantedeschia (arum lily) With its broad arrow-shaped leaves and white arum-like flowers in summer, *Z. aethiopica* is indeed an aristocratic rhizomatous perennial. Even more striking is *Z.* 'Green Goddess' with green, white-splashed spathes.

Plants can be grown in pots of soil-based compost or in a soil bed and should be kept steadily moist all year round. Liquid feed fortnightly in summer. Shade from strong sunshine.

Temporary plants

These plants are discarded when their flower display is over.

Browallia (bush violet) These perennials, which are grown as annual pot plants, produce a profusion of tubular white, blue or lavender flowers in summer.

Sow seeds in early spring and germinate at 65°F (18°C). Can also be sown in late summer for winter flowering. Prick out seedlings into 3 in (8 cm) pots, and pot on as required until plants are in final 5 in (13 cm) pots. Soilless potting compost is recommended. Ensure bright light, but shade from strong sunshine. Water as required. Liquid feed established plants fortnightly in summer.

Celosia (Prince of Wales' feathers) *C. cristata* Plumosa Group has feathery flower heads in summer and autumn, in shades of red, yellow, pink and apricot. They make excellent pot plants and are easily grown from seeds.

Sow early to mid-spring and germinate at 65°F (18°C). Prick out seedlings into 3 in (8 cm) pots and pot on as required until in final

Browallias are temporary pot plants, producing tubular flowers in summer.
Here, *Asparagus densiflorus* 'Sprengeri' makes a pleasing foil

5 in (13 cm) pots. Soilless compost is recommended. Provide bright
light, but shade from strong sunshine. Water as required, avoiding
very wet compost. Liquid feed established plants in summer.
Fuchsia Fuchsia hybrids provide a non-stop display all summer
and into autumn. Depending on habit of growth, they can be
grown as bush plants, as trailers in hanging baskets, or trained to
various forms such as standards, fans and pyramids. (Consult the
Wisley Handbook *Fuchsias* for details of growing and training.)
The trained forms are generally kept for several years, but bush
and basket plants are possibly best renewed each year from
cuttings, discarding the old plants.

To produce bush and basket plants, root soft cuttings in spring
or early summer for flowering plants the following year. Rooting
temperature 65°F (18°C). Start young plants in 3½ in (9 cm) pots
and pot on to final 6-8 in (15-20 cm) pots. Soilless potting compost
is particularly suitable. Pinch out growing tips when plants are
6 in (15 cm) high, and when the resulting lateral shoots are 4 in
(10 cm) long pinch out their tips, too.

Fuchsias should be shaded from strong sun, provided with airy conditions and kept steadily moist. Liquid feed flowering plants fortnightly in summer.

Impatiens (busy lizzie) For their extremely long period of flowering – all summer and into autumn – impatiens have to be regarded as essential conservatory plants. There are various kinds, the seed-raised strains used for bedding making excellent pot plants. Flower colours include shades of red, pink, orange and white. The New Guinea hybrids are particularly attractive as they have bronze foliage.

Seeds are sown in early or mid-spring and germinated in a temperature of 60-65°F (15.6-18.3°C). Impatiens grow well in soilless compost; pot on as necessary. They need copious watering in summer, light shade and high humidity. Liquid feed fortnightly. Discard after flowering.

WARM CONSERVATORY

Permanent plants
Agapetes Attractive flowering shrubs and climbers of which the evergreen climbing *A. macrantha* can be recommended. It has

Agapetes macrantha, an evergreen climber ideally suited to the small conservatory, is particularly valuable as it flowers in winter

Anthurium scherzerianum, left, is an evergreen perennial whose brilliantly coloured spathes will light up a shady part of the conservatory. The distinctive inflorescences of *Aphelandra squarrosa* 'Louisae', right (see p.112), appear in summer and autumn – for the rest of the year enjoy the foliage

pendulous urn-shaped pink or white red-patterned flowers in winter. Height up to 6 ft (1.8 m).

Grow in a pot, tub or bed of humus rich, moisture retentive yet well-drained acid to neutral soil/compost. Succeeds in maximum light or partial shade. Water freely in summer, at which time liquid feed fortnightly, and moderately during winter.

Aglaonema (Chinese evergreen) These low evergreen clump-forming perennials are grown for their handsome broad lance-shaped foliage. There are numerous species, but cultivars of *A. commutatum* are widely grown, the leaves being marked with white or silver.

Grow in beds or pots. Excellent results are obtained in soilless compost. Provide warm humid conditions and a spot out of direct sun for these shade-loving plants. Water as needed in summer, keeping on the dry side in winter. Liquid feed fortnightly in summer.

Anthurium These evergreen perennials create an exotic touch with their colourful spathes: bright scarlet in the species *A. scherzerianum* and scarlet or orange-red in *A. andreanum*. In recent years other colours have appeared such as shades of pink, orange and white.

Provide warm, humid conditions and shade. Grow in pots of soilless compost, watering as needed in summer, but in winter keeping it only slightly moist. Liquid feed fortnightly in summer.

Aphelandra (zebra plant) The perennial *A. squarrosa* 'Louisae' (see p. 111) has large leaves with conspicuous white veins, and pyramid-shaped inflorescences in summer and autumn consisting of bright yellow bracts and small yellow flowers.

Generally grown in pots of soilless or soil-based compost. In warm conditions provide humidity; shade from strong sun; maintain the compost steadily moist; and liquid feed fortnightly in summer. To prevent tall bare stems, cut the plant back by about one-third to half after flowering.

Begonia This is a huge genus, the members of which are ideally suited to the warm conservatory, both flowering and foliage species and hybrids. Of the former there are many attractive kinds like the winter-flowering *B.* × *cheimantha* 'Gloire de Lorraine' and cultivars of *B. hiemalis.* The cane-stemmed begonias, like *B.* × *corallina* which has silver-spotted foliage and pink flowers, can also be recommended. For foliage there are begonias like *B.* × *erythrophylla* whose leaves 'have striking red undersides; *B. serratipetala* with serrated bronzy foliage; and *B. metallica* with bronze-green leaves, red on the underside.

Grow in pots, using soilless compost. Do not allow very wet conditions: ensure compost partially dries out between waterings. Humidity is essential in warm conditions; shade from strong sun but ensure bright light. Liquid feed fortnightly.

Codiaeum (croton) These flamboyant multicoloured evergreen foliage shrubs provide a lush tropical effect to the warm conservatory. Leaf shape, size and colour are variable.

Grow in beds or pots, ideally using soil-based compost in the latter. Pinch out growing tips of young plants to ensure bushy specimens. High temperatures and humidity will ensure lush growth, together with good light, but shade from strong sunshine. Water as needed in summer but cut down in winter. Liquid feed fortnightly in summer.

Cordyline For the warm conservatory the cultivars of *C. fruticosa* (syn. *C. terminalis*) (Ti tree) are recommended. This shrub is evergreen with bold sword-shaped leaves and it can grow quite tall, although slow, eventually making a good specimen plant. There are cultivars with red and green leaves.

Grow in beds or pots, in the latter using soil-based compost. Warmth and humidity are needed together with light shade from the sun. In summer water as required, but in winter water sparingly. Liquid feed fortnightly in summer.

Crotalaria Attractive pea-flowered evergreen shrubs, perennials and annuals. *C. agatiflora* (canary-bird bush) is a 10 ft (3 m) high evergreen shrub with green-yellow flowers in summer and at other times.

Grow in a pot/tub of well drained soil-based compost or in a soil bed. Needs maximum light. Water freely in summer, moderately during winter and liquid feed fortnightly in summer. Reduce old stems by half after flowering.

Ficus The classic conservatory species is *F. benjamina*, the weeping fig, which makes a fine specimen plant when it has attained some height. This small evergreen tree has small leaves, in shape like those of the related rubber plant, rich green and shiny. It has a pendulous habit of growth, unusual among conservatory plants.

Grow in a large pot or tub, using soil-based potting compost. Warm conditions with humidity are needed, together with bright light, but shade from strong sunshine. Water as required in summer, but in winter allow compost to partially dry out between waterings. Liquid feed fortnightly in summer.

Gardenia (Cape jasmine) The evergreen shrub *G. jasminoides* has the most exquisitely fragrant white flowers in the summer and autumn.

Grow in a bed for maximum size (about 6 ft [1.8 m] high), or in a large pot or tub of soil-based potting compost. Growth is also good in soilless compost but it may not be able to support a large plant adequately. Acid to neutral soil is required. Plenty of humidity is needed when temperatures are high, and partial shade. Water as required in summer, but reduce in winter. Liquid feed fortnightly in summer. Young plants should have their growing tips pinched out to induce a bushy habit. After flowering prune back stems by about half their length.

Hymenocallis Bulbs, some evergreen, with daffodil-like scented flowers. *H.* × *macrostephana* is evergreen and produces large white or cream flowers in spring or summer.

Grow in a pot of well drained soil-based compost. Water normally, but reduce considerably in winter – however, avoid drying out. Plants prefer a good level of humidity and light shade from hot sun. Liquid feed in summer. Repot in spring.

Mandevilla These flamboyant evergreen or deciduous climbers produce trumpet-shaped flowers in the spring or summer. The most common species is *Mandevilla splendens* (syn. *Dipladenia splendens*) which provides a long succession of rose-pink flowers during late spring and early summer. It will attain a height of at least 10 ft (3 m).

Grow in a bed or large pot/tub, using well drained soil-based potting compost in the container. High humidity is appreciated in summer together with light shade from strong sun. Water as needed in summer, but in winter only when soil is drying out. If size needs to be contained, prune the plant back hard when flowering is over, cutting the previous season's stems back to within 2 in (5 cm) of their base. Alternatively, if you want a larger plant, leave it unpruned, except for thinning out congested growth as necessary.

Medinilla The spectacular *M. magnifica* is an evergreen shrub about 5 ft (1.5 m) high with deeply veined leaves and pendulous trusses of pink flowers below large pink bracts during spring and summer. Grow in a pot of humus-rich compost, such as a soilless type. Provide partial shade and high humidity; water well in summer, when fortnightly liquid feeding can be carried out, and moderately during winter.

Philodendron For creating a lush jungle-like effect in a warm conservatory, there are few plants to surpass the philodendrons, which are grown for their bold foliage. They are evergreen shrubs and climbers, the latter producing aerial roots on their stems. There are lots to choose from, including the climbers *P. angustisectum* (syn. *P. elegans*) with deeply cut foliage; *P.* 'Burgundy' whose leaves are flushed with red and are wine-red on the undersides; the copper-flushed *P. erubescens*; *P. pedatum* whose glossy oval leaves are dark green; and *P. tuxtlanum* 'Tuxtla' which has glossy foliage. Non-climbing philodendrons include the large-growing *P. pinnatifidum* with wide-spreading deeply cut leaves.

Grow in soil beds or large pots/tubs. Philodendrons like humus-rich soil. A good compost consists of equal parts, by volume, of soil-based and soilless potting compost. Climbing philodendrons are best grown up a moss pole; alternatively train against the back wall of the conservatory. Main requirements are warmth, high humidity and shade from strong sunshine. Water as required in summer, but during winter allow the soil to partially dry out between waterings. Liquid feed fortnightly during summer.

Pycnostachys Attractive bushy perennials with whorls of tubular flowers. *P. dawei* has beautiful bright blue flowers in winter and spring and red-backed foliage. Height up to 5 ft (1.5 m).

Grow in a pot of rich well drained soil-based compost or in a soil bed. Provide maximum light. Water freely in summer, sparingly during winter. Liquid feed fortnightly during growing season.

Pyrostegia The evergreen tendril climber *P. venusta* (flame vine or flower, golden shower) has spectacular golden-orange tubular

Medinilla magnifica, one of the aristocrats of the conservatory, is an evergreen shrub with distinctive foliage and flowers

flowers in clusters from autumn to spring. It quickly attains 30 ft (10 m).

Grow in a large pot/tub of rich well drained soil-based compost or, even better, in a soil bed. Ensure maximum light, humidity, water freely in very warm conditions, but reduce in lower temperatures. Liquid feed fortnightly in summer. If congested, thin out older stems after flowering.

Sanchezia Evergreen shrubs, climbers and perennials, attractive flowering and foliage plants. The 5 ft (1.5 m) tall shrub *S. speciosa* is grown mainly for its large glossy yellow-veined leaves. Tubular yellow flowers with red bracts are produced in summer.

Grow in a pot/tub of soil-based compost, or in a soil bed, ensuring good drainage. Water freely in summer, but reduce in winter. Liquid feed fortnightly during summer. Thrives in maximum light or partial shade, and high humidity.

Solandra Evergreen climbers with big and spectacular trumpet-shaped flowers. *S. maxima* (golden-chalice vine, capa de oro) (see p. 118), is a strong grower to 30 ft (10 m) or more, and produces scented yellow flowers during spring and summer.

Grow in a rich, well-drained soil: pot/tub of soil-based compost or, better, soil bed. Ensure maximum light. Water freely in summer, sparingly during winter. High humidity. Liquid feed fortnightly in summer. If congested, thin out older stems after flowering.

Stephanotis (Madagascar jasmine) The evergreen climber *S. floribunda* produces clusters of white waxy flowers between spring and autumn, which give off a delightfully strong fragrance. It is a vigorous plant, capable of attaining at least 15 ft (5 m) in height.

Grow in a soil bed or large pot or tub. As it likes a humus-rich soil, a soilless potting compost can be used in containers. A humus rich soil-based compost would also be suitable. Train stems to the back wall of the conservatory. Water as required throughout the year and provide fortnightly liquid feeds in summer. Shade lightly from strong sun and provide moderate humidity around the plant. If it is necessary to restrict size, prune the plant in late winter. The main stems and the side shoots can be cut back.

Tecoma Attractive flowering evergreen shrubs and trees. *T. stans* (syn. *Bignonia stans, Stenolobium stans*) (yellow bells or yellow elder) (see p. 118) has ferny foliage and pendulous clusters of yellow trumpet-shaped flowers between spring and autumn.

Grow in a large pot/tub of well drained soil-based compost or in a soil bed. Provide maximum light. Moderate watering in summer, very sparing during winter. Liquid feed fortnightly in summer. Prune after flowering to reduce height.

Tetranema Attractive flowering perennials. *T. roseum* (syn. *T. mexicanum*) (Mexican foxglove, Mexican violet), is a small plant with purple foxglove-like flowers on and off for most of the year.

Grow in pots of well drained soil-based compost. Water normally in summer, sparingly during winter. Avoid over-wet conditions. Liquid feed fortnightly in summer. Needs good light, but shade from sunshine, and a humid atmosphere.

PLANTS FOR SHADY CONSERVATORIES

We have seen under Choosing and Siting that a very sunny position is not essential, as success can be achieved in shade. There are certainly many plants that will enjoy or tolerate shade. Bear in mind there are many more suitable plants.

Cool conservatory

Permanent plants – **Camellias** will succeed in shady conservatories, especially as it is recommended they are stood outdoors in a partially shady place for the summer.

Temporary plants – Hardy **Bulbs** for winter and spring flowering do not need sun in order to create a display. One can also include **Lilium** (lilies) here; they should flower in sunless conditions. **Primula** species actually enjoy cool shady conditions so should be high on the list of suitable plants.

Intermediate conservatory

Permanent plants – **Bromeliads,** although they like good light, will succeed without any sun (they come from tropical rain forests which are often very gloomy within). **Ferns** are shade lovers, so use plenty in the sunless conservatory. **Palms** and **Tibouchina** should succeed without any sun, although they do like good light. The bushy evergreen perennial **Impatiens** needs good light, but shade from sun.

Temporary plants – **Fuchsias** are worth trying, as I have found they flower reasonably well in a sunless position, though it must be said not as prolifically as those in sunnier conditions. **Impatiens** perform very well in shade for me, flowering their heads off, so are highly recommended.

Warm conservatory

Permanent plants – **Aglaonema** species (Chinese evergreens) are shade lovers and will succeed in the warm sunless conservatory where they will create a foil for flowering plants such as **Anthurium** species with their colourful long-lasting flower spathes. **Begonia** species, for flowers and foliage, succeed in shade although good light is essential, and there is a very wide range to choose from. **Philodendron** species will succeed without sun as they are 'jungle' plants. Again there is a big selection of these foliage plants available. **Sanchezia,** evergreen shrubs, climbers and perennials thrive in maximum light or partial shade.

Caring for Plants

Conservatory plants need caring for properly and on a regular basis if they are to grow well. This means:

- Pot and feed when required.
- Pay attention to watering.
- Provide the right atmosphere and other growing conditions.
- Prune, if required.
- Control pests and diseases.

COMPOSTS AND POTTING

In the descriptive lists suitable types of potting compost have been recommended. For most permanent plants soil-based compost is recommended: John Innes potting compost. JIP1 is used for initial potting of young plants, JIP2 for potting on, and JIP3 when planting in large pots or tubs.

Soilless composts are recommended for some plants, especially temporary pot plants and permanent kinds that like humus-rich soil, and these imply peat-based or the new peatless composts.

Plastic pots are widely used for growing conservatory plants (especially temporary pot plants), but for larger specimens I recommend the heavier clay pots as they are more stable. Plants should be potted on as required, generally before they become pot-bound (pots packed full of roots). Plants are often moved on two sizes – for example, from a 4 in (10 cm) to a 6 in (15 cm) pot – although very slow-growing plants should be moved on one size each time.

Eventually many permanent plants, like shrubs, trees and perennials, will need to go into final containers. These may be large pots, maybe ornamental kinds, or wooden tubs, the square Versailles design being particularly attractive in conservatories. Final containers will vary in size but should be a minimum of 12 in (30 cm) in diameter and depth, through to 18 in (45 cm) or more, depending on size of plant.

Plenty of headroom is needed for the vigorous climber *Solandra maxima*, above (see p. 116), whose huge scented flowers are produced during spring and summer. *Tecoma stans*, below (see p. 116), is a large shrub with attractive ferny foliage and produces trumpet-shaped flowers between spring and autumn

Permanent plants are best potted on annually in early spring. Temporary pot plants may need moving on throughout the growing season as well.

Drainage material is often dispensed with these days but I feel it is necessary when using pots over 6 in (15 cm) in diameter and certainly for final containers. 'Crocks' or broken clay pots still provide the best drainage material and the layer should be covered with rough leafmould or something similar before adding compost. Make sure you leave watering space at the top of the pot or container – from ½ in (12 mm) to 1 in (2.5 cm) according to size.

Repotting

Plants in final containers will need to have some of their compost replaced every couple of years or so as it starts to deteriorate. This involves repotting into the same container in early spring.

Remove the plant from the container and reduce the size of the root ball by at least 2 in (5 cm) all round by teasing away compost and root pruning if necessary. Then replace in the same container – which should have been cleaned out and be perfectly dry – and work fresh compost all around the root ball, right down to the bottom.

In the interim years simply top dress with fresh compost after removing the top 1 in (2.5 cm) or so.

PLANTING

Planting in raised beds is the same as planting container-grown plants outdoors. Simply make a hole slightly larger than the root ball, remove the plant from its pot carefully to avoid root disturbance, place it in the centre of the hole, work fine soil around it and firm well. The top of the root ball should be covered with about ½ in (12 mm) of soil. With container-grown plants planting can be carried out at any time of year.

Finish off by mulching the surface of the soil about 2 in (5 cm) deep with pulverised bark or coconut fibre.

PLUNGING

This attractive method of displaying plants in pots ensures a humid atmosphere around them. Plunging is recommended for displaying groups of plants in planters (large deep floor containers), or single plants in ornamental pot holders.

Nidularium fulgens (see p.104) is one of the more flamboyant bromeliads, bringing a touch of the tropical rain forest to the intermediate conservatory

The pots are plunged up to their rims in water-absorbing horticultural aggregate or coconut fibre, which is then kept constantly moist to provide atmospheric humidity.

WATERING

Specific watering needs have been given for the plants in the descriptive lists. Plants do vary in their water requirements, some having to be kept steadily moist all year round, others relishing plenty of water in the growing period (spring and summer), but far less in autumn and winter when they are resting.

There are various ways of determining when water is required. The usual technique is to push a finger down into the compost. If during the growing period it is dry on top and moist below, then water is needed. However, if moist or wet on the surface do not water. If during the resting period (when we may need to water more sparingly, keeping the compost only slightly moist), the compost surface is dry and it feels dryish lower down, water can be applied. Then leave alone until the compost is drying out again.

When watering always completely fill the space between the rim of the pot and the surface of the compost to ensure the entire depth of compost is moistened.

Test soil beds in the same way, but this time apply enough water to penetrate to a depth of at least 6 in (15 cm): approximately nearly 5 gallons per square yard (27 litres per square metre).

Soil or compost may also be tested for water requirements with the aid of a soil-moisture meter.

Some conservatory plants prefer soft (lime-free) water, especially lime-hating plants (those that need acid compost or soil) and bromeliads. Rainwater is ideal for these.

HUMIDITY

Many conservatory plants relish a humid or moist atmosphere in warm conditions – say from 60°F (15.5°C) upwards – and some need very high humidity, particularly many of the tropical foliage plants. This is indicated in the descriptive lists. Some plants, however, need dry air all year round, including desert cacti and succulents and pelargoniums.

Humidity should not be provided in cool conditions – once the temperature drops below about 50°F (10°C) – as then the air must be kept as dry as possible.

In the lived-in conservatory humidity has to be provided locally around the plants – no one wants to live in rain-forest conditions, and it would do the furnishings no good at all. Local humidity can be provided by plunging plants (see p. 120) or by mist spraying the leaves several times a day with soft tap water or rain water. Do not mist spray hairy or woolly plants, though. In a conservatory devoted purely to plants, one can damp down the floor and staging twice a day, morning and evening.

On staging, gravel trays filled with horticultural aggregate will provide local humidity if the aggregate is kept moist.

VENTILATION

Ventilation is needed all year round to maintain fresh healthy conditions in the conservatory. It can also be used to help reduce temperature and humidity. Ventilation should always be consistent with maintaining the temperature required.

Effective ventilation is provided by opening roof ventilators and side windows or vents. Then the warm air rises and escapes through the conservatory roof and draws in cool air from lower levels.

SHADING

During the spring and summer shading will be needed by plants and people. Hot sun shining through the glass can scorch plants badly. Shading will also help to keep the temperature down and can be used in conjunction with ventilation.

Ideally provide shade only when the sun is shining, removing it at other times to ensure plants receive maximum light.

There are some groups of plants, though, that do not need shading. These include the desert cacti and succulents, perhaps not the ideal choice for the conservatory that is also used as a living room and contains plants that need shade.

Do not use shading in autumn and winter, as then plants need maximum light. While on this subject, do remember to keep the glass scrupulously clean to ensure optimum light transmission. This, again, is especially important in autumn and winter.

FEEDING PLANTS

Conservatory plants need feeding between mid-spring and early autumn (the growing period), never between mid-autumn and early spring when they may be resting or growth has slowed down. Never feed newly potted or repotted plants as the fresh compost will keep them going until new roots have permeated it – about eight weeks on average. Never feed plants if the soil or compost is dry – moisten it first.

During the growing period fortnightly liquid feeding is ideal for most potted plants, using a houseplant fertilizer based on seaweed. There are fertilizers formulated for foliage and flowering plants.

To cut down on frequency of feeding, consider using fertilizer tablets for potted plants, these being pushed into the compost where they slowly release their nutrients over several weeks.

Plants in soil beds can be fed by lightly forking a dry general-purpose fertilizer into the soil surface in mid-spring. This can be followed by monthly liquid feeds during summer if you feel plant growth needs a boost.

PRUNING

In the descriptive lists specific details of pruning have been given where required. Here we will look at the general principles.

Use a pair of very sharp secateurs for pruning to ensure really clean, smooth cuts which heal quickly.

Pruning cuts should always be made just above growth buds, which are situated in the axils between leaf stalks and stems. Never leave a portion of stem above a bud, or this will die back, and do not make the cut so near the bud that it is damaged.

Any large pruning cuts on shrubs – 1 in (2.5 cm) or more in

Citrus aurantium, the Seville orange (see p.106). Even if the temperature is not high enough for fruiting, citrus make handsome evergreen foliage plants

diameter – should be treated with a proprietary pruning compound to prevent diseases from entering.

Not all plants require regular pruning by any means, but occasional attention may be required. Cut back any dead and dying growth to live wood as required. Dead flowers should be removed to maintain a tidy appearance and prevent infection from botrytis.

PESTS AND DISEASES

Aphids
Greenfly are the most common aphids found under glass. They feed in colonies on tender shoot tips and leaves, sucking the sap which weakens the plant and distorts growth. Spray with derris, pyrethrum or an insecticidal soap as soon as noticed.

Botrytis (grey mould)
This is the most common fungal disease, attacking a wide range of plants, causing parts to rot. It takes the form of a grey mould on

flowers, leaves and stems and in the right conditions can spread rapidly. To prevent it, avoid very damp conditions and provide plenty of ventilation. Control botrytis by spraying plants with a carbendazim fungicide (ideally taking them outdoors). Also cut off affected parts of plants.

Glasshouse red spider mite

Microscopic yellowish-green or reddish spider-like creatures, which feed on leaves resulting in fine pale mottling, can be deterred by mist spraying leaves daily with plain water. Spray with malathion, pirimiphos-methyl or dimethoate as soon as noticed. Alternatively try biological control, using the predatory mite *Phytoseiulus persimilis* (do not use pesticides where biological controls have been introduced).

Mealybug

These soft grey-white plant bugs with a white woolly covering feed on the stems of many plants, especially woody kinds. Dab pests with an artist's brush dipped in methylated spirits, or spray plants with malathion or pirimiphos-methyl. Biological control with a ladybird, *Cryptolaemus montrouzieri*, can reduce infestations during the summer.

Mildew, powdery

A fungal disease appearing as a white powdery deposit on leaves and shoot tips of many plants, often causes distorted growth. Spray affected plants with triforine or carbendazim fungicide (ideally taking them outdoors).

Scale insects

These generally brownish insects, resembling shells and immobile, feed on stems and leaves of many plants, especially woody kinds. Spray plants with malathion or pirimiphos-methyl.

Whitefly

Tiny white winged insects with flat oval scale-like nymphs congregate in colonies on the undersides of leaves of many conservatory plants, where they suck the sap. As soon as noticed, spray with permethrin, pyrethrum or an insecticidal soap. Alternatively try biological control, using the parasitic wasp *Encarsia formosa*. Do not use pesticides where biological control has been introduced.

Effective Displays

Owning a conservatory provides an excellent opportunity of creating some imaginative plant displays. Somehow, potted plants simply stood on the staging without much thought do not look right in the relatively grand surroundings of a conservatory – a much better effect is achieved if they are grouped together, and especially if they contrast in colour, shape and texture. Remember that all plants in a group should require the same conditions such as temperature and light.

It has already been mentioned in the chapter on Fixtures and Fittings that tiered staging allows one to create impressive and professional-looking plant displays, especially with the liberal use of trailing plants. But using staging is not the only way of displaying potted plants. Groups can be created on the floor, too, such as matching ones either side of the conservatory or interior door, or semi-circular groups in the corners.

The following ideas show how some of the plants in the descriptive lists can be used effectively, plus a few extras for adding the finishing touches.

SEASONAL GROUPS

In the conservatories and greenhouses of many private and public gardens you will find that seasonal plant groups are popular. Why not reflect the different seasons in your conservatory with appropriate pot plants? Here is a taster of the countless possibilities.

Cool conservatory

The cool conservatory in spring could feature camellias. Surround these with pots of spring bulbs like narcissus and hyacinths, and pots of the greenhouse primulas *P. malacoides* or *P. obconica.*

For summer colour try bold groups of regal pelargoniums, with a foil of *Chlorophytum comosum* 'Variegatum', the ubiquitous but

A spring group which features daffodils, silver-leaved cyclamen and primulas – an ideal plant association in a cool conservatory

useful spider plant with green and white striped grassy foliage.

Autumn could bring bold groups of charm chrysanthemums, which do not really need any other plants with them.

Intermediate conservatory
Bush fuchsias, with standards to give height, make impressive groups for summer-long colour. Foliage plants create an excellent foil, such as the variegated abutilons *A.* × *hybridum* 'Savitzii' and *A. striatum* 'Thompsonii'.

Celosia cristata Plumosa Group is a favourite display plant, its brilliant feathery flower heads produced over a long period in summer and autumn contrasting beautifully with 'cool' ferns such as *Pteris tremula* and *Asplenium bulbiferum*.

Strelitzia reginae (see p.101), an evergreen perennial, takes five to seven years to reach flowering size – but it is worth the wait, and it has good foliage

PERMANENT GROUPS

Try to group permanent plants together as attractively as possible, using flowering and foliage kinds. This is quite easily achieved whether plants are in pots or soil beds. For instance, in the **cool** conservatory a group consisting of *Clivia miniata*, *Lantana camara* and *Strelitzia reginae* offers plenty of contrast, especially in shape.

In the **intermediate** conservatory, foliage plants like ferns, together with zantedeschia or arum lily, can be grouped around such plants as brunfelsia and hibiscus to create attractive groups.

In the **warm** conservatory, one can create some really colourful and flamboyant groups with tropical flowering and foliage plants. Creating single-colour groups can be fun, such as a red group using, for example, anthuriums with red spathes, codiaeums with a predominance of red in their leaves, red-leaved cordylines and perhaps the red-flushed *Philodendron* 'Burgundy'. Here there will also be dramatic contrast in leaf shape.

CREATING HEIGHT

For some inexplicable reason, home gardeners often fail to achieve adequate height in groups of plants, arranging them all on one level thereby creating flat-looking displays. Professional gardeners invariably elevate some of the plants in groups to create height. For instance, in floor displays that are viewed all round, the plants in the centre could be tall, or elevated, gradually grading to shorter material towards the edges. This could create, for instance, a pyramid or cone shape.

When arranging plants on ordinary bench-type staging, place tall (or elevated) specimens at the back and again gradually grade down to the front with shorter plants.

How does one create height? Either use taller plants, or elevate plants on upturned flower pots. Also, one can use climbers to create height in groups, such as philodendrons on moss poles in the warm conservatory.

If one needs to hide pots, such as those used to elevate plants, then fill in with pots of trailing foliage plants such as small-leaved hardy ivies (cultivars of *Hedera helix*) which are very adaptable and can be used in any temperature, or *Asparagus densiflorus* 'Sprengeri' (a favourite of the professionals and suited to the intermediate or warm conservatory).

A useful trick to help in hiding pots, and so on, is to slightly tilt the pots of trailers forwards. They can be supported with little blocks of wood, or something similar. Obviously they have to be stood upright for watering, but it is often worth the effort to achieve a professional-looking display.

TRAILING PLANTS

Apart from their obvious role in elevated containers, trailing plants are very useful for including around or along the edge of groups, particularly those arranged on staging. They can be used to hide edges of staging and pots. Ivies and asparagus have already been mentioned; others to consider are: *Epipremnum aureum* cultivars with marbled foliage, warm conservatory; *Ficus pumila*, the creeping fig, with green leaves, intermediate or warm; *Oplismenus hirtellus* 'Variegatus', green and white striped grass, intermediate or warm; and *Stenotaphrum secundatum* 'Variegatum', a cream and green striped grass, intermediate or warm.

SPECIMEN PLANTS

Large specimen plants are very much in vogue for interior landscaping and particularly popular are tall bare-stemmed plants with a tuft of leaves at the top, such as large yuccas and dracaenas. Large specimens create a sense of maturity in a conservatory and make impressive focal points when positioned in corners or each side of doors. Palms are enjoying renewed popularity (they were in vogue during the Victorian period). It is possible to buy large specimens of numerous species, including those mentioned in the descriptive lists – *Howeia forsteriana* (thatch-leaf palm) and *Phoenix canariensis* (Canary Island date palm), both for the intermediate conservatory.

In warm conditions *Cordyline fruticosa* cultivars (Ti tree) and the ubiquitous *Ficus benjamina* (weeping fig) make excellent specimen plants. One could also use climbing philodendrons trained to moss poles. Although not included in the lists, *Yucca elephantipes* deserves a mention here. It develops a thick trunk supporting at the top a rosette of green, erect sword-like leaves, and is suitable for the intermediate or warm conservatory.

This display of tropical foliage plants in a warm conservatory has been elevated by means of tiered wooden staging

The Small Greenhouse

- DEENAGH GOOLD-ADAMS -
revised by RAY WAITE

A small greenhouse can be used for display, as well as for propagating and bringing on plants for the home

Introduction

There is no mystery in the management of a greenhouse. Regular attention and common sense are the basis of all success under glass, while the application of intelligence, ingenuity or expenditure can overcome most problems if time is in short supply! The one essential is a will to grow plants, not just look at them. The key questions are 'Do you want a greenhouse?' and 'Why?'

The greenhouse must give pleasure and fulfil a role, even if this is one that is not recognised by the neighbours or indeed by the family, let alone by any horticultural expert. A greenhouse is a very personal thing and difficult to share, although its maintenance does sometimes demand the cooperation of others.

Today the conservatory has become fashionable as well as useful and is another option. A lean-to greenhouse may be used as a conservatory and is often the cheapest way of extending the home.

To have a small greenhouse is not one of life's major decisions. It is a fringe benefit that may cost more than some wish to spend on a hobby, but it should not cause any more difficulties than buying a freezer or a washing machine.

The fact that every healthy plant grows bigger every day is an everlasting problem. It is sometimes solved by using the greenhouse as a production unit, or as a staging post for plants that will decorate the garden or the home when full grown. There is always an element of this. Some people are only attracted by rare plants whereas others are equally devoted to familiar flowers. Anticipation is probably the keenest pleasure in growing plants, and the increasing skill and knowledge that can be gathered through life is perhaps the greatest satisfaction. Seed sowing and propagation are essential to a lasting interest in a greenhouse and make this form of gardening an enjoyable and inexpensive hobby.

As far as pot plants are concerned the greenhouse can be a nursery, a forcing house, a display centre or, alas, a casualty ward and convalescent home. The more knowledgeable and enthusiastic one becomes, the harder it is to limit and rationalise the use of glass; and this often leads to there being not one small greenhouse

The colourful annual *Schizanthus pinnatus* hybrids are easily raised from seed sown in spring or late summer

but two or three, when one large one would have been so much easier to manage.

It is a sound idea to start with a mixed collection. In fact it is almost unavoidable; there are many plants so prodigal of seed or easily rooted cuttings that they pass from hand to hand and turn up in most collections.

Although it may seem less than friendly to look a gift-horse in the mouth, it is madness not to examine a gift plant closely before adding it to your collection. A hand lens is helpful for identifying pests; the tender growing points and the backs of the leaves are the places to look. In any case, two weeks isolation is a wise precaution and good hygiene should always be practised. In a mixed greenhouse or conservatory one hopes to avoid a serious build-up of the pests that are attracted by any one plant family. There is also more scope for a continuous rather than seasonal display.

The true plantsman who sees each plant individually may not be concerned with the general display at all. The only consideration will be the choice of position of light, shade, warmth and air to suit each treasure best. For there is quite a divergence of micro-climates even in small greenhouses. Unhappy plants are worth moving and there should also be no hesitation in examining the roots. It does no harm to knock a plant cleanly out of its pot and replace it, and much can be learnt. Any seriously ailing plant should be discarded completely, unless it is particularly rare or valuable – better by far to make room to grow another specimen to its full potential.

In the very limited space of the small greenhouse or conservatory there is no room to grow a large number of plants perfectly. Indeed half a dozen exhibition plants might fill it. One way to overcome this difficulty is the use of hanging baskets, pots and shelves to create layers of growth.

Another is to concentrate on the 'mini' plant. These have greatly multiplied in recent times, as the need to transport flowering plants by road in cardboard containers hastened the development of compact selections of the most popular plants. Calceolarias, cinerarias, cyclamen, chrysanthemums, gloxinias, saintpaulias and pelargoniums are just some of those that have been induced to concentrate their charms, and together they cover every season. Other plants are naturally small or propagated yearly from small pieces. The enormous and enduring popularity of fuchsias, chrysanthemums and pelargoniums is partly due to the fact that, as they become unmanageably large, they can be replaced by young cuttings taking up much less room.

Another way of saving space is to confine everything to pots too

Near-hardy nerines make a fine autumn display in an unheated greenhouse with their lily-like flowers

small for full development. With careful feeding this can be remarkably successful but it does not suit either every plant or every person. Some of us wish to grow the best and discard those that do not meet our high standards.

All greenhouses are much the same in summer, depending only on the management of ventilation, humidity and shading for their differing climates. The key questions for year-long interest are what plants can be over-wintered and how early in the year active growth starts. Many plants have a natural rest at a much lower temperature than for their normal growth, while some, like fuchsias, will either rest or grow according to the temperature. Others will grow in winter and rest in summer if given suitable conditions. Many greenhouse plants come from the southern hemisphere and some can be persuaded that a dry rest in our winter corresponds to the summer drought of their homeland.

The final choice of what to grow will depend on the temperature that is maintained in winter. Without any heat at all the scope for an all-the-year round display is limited by the fact that a plant that is not frost-resistant cannot be guaranteed to survive. All the same a lean-to against a south wall can be very rewarding, and spring comes much earlier under any form of glass.

The so-called 'cold' greenhouse means exactly that and will not

Coleus (left) are excellent foliage plants, though shortlived; *Acacia armata* (right) is one of the best small shrubs for the greenhouse and grows about 10 ft (3 m) high

maintain frost-free conditions during really severe weather. However, precautions can be taken to protect hardier plants by using layers of newspaper or sacking. Even then there are limitations on the range of plants that can be over-wintered.

If a minimum winter temperature between 4°C (40°F) and 7°C (45°F) is assured, the greenhouse is usually called 'cool'. This is the most popular form of heated greenhouse. All such greenhouses become easier to manage in winter with every extra degree of heat, although the virtual doubling of the cost of fuel with every extra 2.8°C (5°F) is a powerful deterrent.

Traditionally the cool greenhouse became 'intermediate' when the minimum temperature maintained was 13°C (55°F), but today 'warm' seems a more suitable term and the only question is the definition of warmth. There is a tendency for warmth to begin at 10°C (50°F) in rather the same spirit that life begins at 40! In other words, hope springs eternal and some tropical plants will survive although they are happier at 13°C (55°F). This last temperature is the highest that amateurs generally aim at in the free-standing greenhouse. Where there is a conservatory against a house wall connected with the central heating system, higher temperatures may prevail and the tropical plants we call house plants can be freely grown.

Site and Structure

An amateur greenhouse of up to 1000 cubic feet (28 m³) does not usually interest the planning authorities, unless it is on a boundary or attached to a building. The local building inspector will have to approve any structure being added to a house and there are regulations about size and use so that it is advisable to check the position locally. If you are a tenant, remember that once fixed to a permanent concrete or brick base, the greenhouse is no longer a tenant's fixture.

Some greenhouses are erected directly on the ground while others have portable base plates of concrete, wood or metal. A really solid base does add to the life of the structure and it is obvious that, if in time the building sags, the glass is likely to crack and leaks will develop. The glass needs to be set in some soft material (putty is no longer used) to avoid leaks and loss of heat in winter.

The materials of which greenhouses are made vary in popularity as their costs and ease of maintenance increase or decrease. It is never difficult to find a possible scientific advantage for either a new or cheaper material. Yet everyone has a preference for wood or metal, regardless of its intrinsic merit, and it is a pity to spend one's leisure in a building one dislikes.

In some settings the traditional white painted softwood is so much more visually satisfying that it must be preferred for a conservatory. Nevertheless the cost of frequent painting needs to be faced. The glazing bars of even a wooden conservatory will probably be of aluminium today.

The most popular wood, known as western red cedar, is a rot-resisting softwood from North America. This wood, from the tree *Thuja plicata*, is usually stained with a solution to make it water-proof and retain the natural red colour. Another method of keeping the wood in good condition is a yearly treatment with thick penetrating oil.

The aluminium alloy greenhouses so popular today need less maintenance than wood, but vary greatly in quality both in design and strength. They can also be had in anodised colour which can have a bronzed appearance or in white vinyl-covered aluminium.

Although metal is colder than wood this is not of serious con-sequence in small lightly constructed buildings. Wood is more convenient when it comes to fixing up shading material or a plastic

A traditional wooden greenhouse at the RHS Garden, Wisley

lining. Maximum light in winter is vital, but this is affected more by the position of the greenhouse than its construction nowadays. An east-west orientation is best for winter light but in a very small building this does not make much difference.

A lean-to built against a wall saves some fuel in winter; but it receives less light and is more difficult to ventilate efficiently than the ordinary span-roofed type. A good choice in certain circumstances is a three-quarter span. This over-tops a wall and has two-way ridge ventilation but is an expensive option as it has to be custom-built. A south wall is regarded as the best position, though very hot in summer. Nevertheless, a lean-to on any wall is possible, with a west-facing situation being quite adequate for a wide range of plants during the summer. Sometimes lack of space makes a round or hexagonal greenhouse the best choice.

Transparent films are an alternative to glass. The simplest structure is a walk-in polythene tunnel which, although not particularly attractive, can be used to grow many edible crops and some flowers. There is now available a conventionally styled greenhouse, which has an aluminium structure and is double-glazed with the newer films. It is claimed that these are superior to glass with regard to light transmission. The double glazing is an obvious fuel-saver and also helps to enhance temperatures in a cold greenhouse during spring and autumn, thus extending the growing season.

If a greenhouse is on a solid base, it is less suitable for growing plants in the ground. Brick walls up to the staging save fuel, but are now rare because of the cost of the brickwork. A substantial wooden base is some substitute, but plastic panels do not save fuel unless thick insulating material is fitted inside them. As many additional plants can be grown under the staging when there is glass to the ground, a panelled base can be a false economy.

It is not possible to find all the virtues in one ready-made structure, but it is well worth comparing one with another. The Chelsea and large provincial flower shows are good places to examine a variety of greenhouses and conservatories. As the available site may affect the choice this needs to be considered first. The distance from a source of electricity is important even if it is not going to be used for heating.

Lighting, fans, seed-raisers, mist propagation and power drills are just some of the many extras using electricity. If natural gas is to be used for heating or if an outside oil tank or fuel store will be needed, this is the time to decide where they will be. Mains water is also helpful, even though rain water is often preferred to tap water. Automatic watering may need mains water pressure or a water tank at least 3 ft (90 cm) above the staging.

If plants are to be grown in the ground, the soil must be fairly well

An aluminium greenhouse at the Chelsea Show

A greenhouse at Wisley with an aluminium frame covered in transparent film

drained and this is more easily attended to before the greenhouse is put up.

A position that is open to winter sunlight and not over-shadowed by trees or buildings is the aim, and one does not want a hedge or fence too close although shelter from wind is important. There is some conflict of opinion as to which way to align the greenhouse, though this may be determined by the site. For the small greenhouse, alignment is not that critical (as stated above), but I favour a north-south orientation.

Here are some points to look for when choosing a small greenhouse or conservatory:

- Method and amount of ventilation and whether it can be automated. Extra ventilation is almost always essential as when the ventilators are open they should equal at least one fifth of the floor area and ideally open to an angle of 50°.
- General stability and likely wind resistance if the site is exposed.
- Foundations required and method of construction.
- Strength and height of staging provided and whether it is suitable for your purposes. Much gravel, clay pots or sand capillary benches can be heavy. One needs an absolutely flat surface for all capillary watering.
- Removal of excess condensation. Make sure there is an adequate channel on the glazing bars to achieve this.
- Width of entrance and height of sill. Also ensure that the door has strong fixings and opens easily.
- Check terms if manufacturers deliver and erect, and look at 'Do it yourself' building instructions.
- Make sure glass and base plate are included in the price and discover if they will be delivered with the greenhouse.

If a greenhouse is put up on grass, the turf should be removed with an inch of top soil and stacked to make potting soil. However, the busy gardener may feel more inclined to cover the grass with black plastic sheeting until it is dead and then cultivate the soil or remove it for use elsewhere. If plants are grown in the ground, the soil is managed much as in the open garden, bearing in mind that it does not have the benefit of frost or rain. A friable loam containing plenty of organic matter is the aim.

When ground is not cultivated, the floor inside the greenhouse can be treated in various ways. On a wet site concrete is probably the best. For retaining moisture in summer, when the floor is sprayed to increase the humidity, rammed soil or ash with a duck-board path has been the traditional working arrangement. A central path of paving blocks with gravel on the soil under the benches is more attractive. A conservatory often looks best if the same paving as the terrace continues inside or alternatively if the flooring in the house is carried through to the conservatory. This is not always practical. Wall to wall carpeting cannot be 'damped down' and vinyl tiles can be death traps when wet. Where a solid floor is constructed insulation with polystyrene sheeting can be of value, since 8 per cent of heat is lost downwards.

The actual foundations of a free-standing greenhouse should rest on firm sub-soil. When laying concrete or brick foundations, leave entry points for electric cables and water pipes. Pieces of hose do well for this, although I once found that a pygmy vole took up residence as a result!

A greenhouse is really incomplete without a cold frame. This is an intermediate stage for hardening off plants before planting them outside. Alternatively plants can be grown in the frame before bringing them in to frost-free conditions.

A cold frame is essential if one is to make the most of a greenhouse

Heating, Ventilation and Shading

HEATING

The cost of heating has multiplied so many times in recent years that we hesitate before deciding to heat a greenhouse at all. At the same time the savings made by raising, preserving and propagating our own plants have also greatly increased.

An amateur's collection of plants can be irreplaceable, costly to replace, or almost valueless; so the cost of installing and running an efficient heating system during a severe winter may be either well worthwhile or quite unacceptable.

A cold greenhouse will only protect hardy plants from wind and rain, but this is not usually the aim. Most of us have a mixture of tender plants and want some to be decorative at all seasons. This is even more true of a conservatory attached to the house. Few plants mind a brief drop in temperature so long as they do not freeze, especially if this happens during a fairly dormant growth period.

The cost of heating will vary with the region of the country and elevation of the site. Exposure, too, is an important factor, for heat loss can double with winds blowing at 15 mph (24 km ph). Insulation will of course help, but it must be as complete as possible for maximum effect. Various transparent films which provide double glazing have become popular, especially now that plastic studs and other fixings are obtainable for aluminium greenhouses. Bubble plastic is particularly efficient and, although it reduces light transmission, this is unlikely to be detrimental to the normal range of plants grown. Plastic film also is a convenient material for partitioning a greenhouse, so that only a small area needs to be heated. Taking this a stage further, a propagating frame will give very comfortable conditions for small plants.

A simple calculation can be used to gain a fairly accurate idea of the heat required to keep temperatures at an acceptable level. No allowance need be made for the differences in heat loss through various materials. First, measure the total surface area of roof, sides and floor, including any small walls and doors. Secondly, decide on the temperature lift required. This is the difference between the lowest temperature likely to be experienced in a given area and the minimum temperature necessary for the plants concerned. With this information, calculate thus:

Area in square feet × temperature lift in °F × 1.4 = Btu/hour

or

$$\frac{\text{Area in metres}^2 \times \text{temperature lift in °C} \times 7.9}{1000} = \text{kWatt}$$

(3412 Btu = 1 kWatt)

The resultant figure, rounded up, will give the output required from a given heat source.

Greenhouses can be heated by natural or bottled gas, solid fuel, paraffin or electricity. The latter is now the cheapest when thermostatically controlled fan heaters are used.

Natural gas heaters can be very good, but as with the simple paraffin types, the greenhouse should be slightly ventilated at all times so that any injurious gases and excess condensation can be dissipated. Gas heaters can usually be modified to burn bottled gas. Thermostatic control is not available on all models and even then most rely on non-electric operation.

Electric heaters should always be fitted with a thermostat. To give accurate control, the thermostat should be aspirated and sited in the centre of the greenhouse. However, small fan heaters usually have the thermostat incorporated in the unit itself. A recent survey has shown that electric tubular heaters are not very economical in terms either of initial outlay or running costs.

There is no doubt that traditional hot water pipes are still the best for a larger greenhouse, particularly if it is joined to the house, when the central heating system can be extended. A free-standing separate boiler requires more attention, especially if solid fuel is used. Oil and gas as heat sources can be very convenient and automatically controlled.

Whatever the system, there will always be cold and warm spots, although these can be used to advantage. A maximum and minimum thermometer will record what is actually happening in various positions. Different temperature zones will be very noticeable with gas or paraffin heaters, while electric fan heaters tend to give more even heat distribution.

VENTILATION

Heating is only part of the control of climate under glass and to create good growing conditions it is also necessary to adjust to the prevailing weather. Even in midwinter during a cold spell, sun shining on glass can raise the temperature appreciably and as the season progresses heat can become excessive. The trapped warmth

145

does not escape as quickly as it is gained, so ventilation may be necessary at any time. Rapid fluctuations in temperature should always be guarded against, but this is much more difficult in small greenhouses where the volume of air is not large.

For a few people with leisure, it may be a pleasure to keep a constant eye on the weather and wind direction, so that green-house ventilation can be adjusted accordingly. For most gardeners, this is impractical, but it is possible to reach some sort of compromise. In any case, it is much better to give more ventilation when leaving for the day in spring, summer and autumn, even if temperatures go down somewhat.

Simple automatic ventilator openers can be fitted. These consist of a cylinder filled with a waxy substance that expands and contracts with the temperature and in turn moves a piston up and down, thus opening and closing the ventilators. They can be sluggish in action but are a good first line of defence and need not be fitted to every opening. Much more sophisticated electrically operated equipment is also available.

Extractor fans are useful. They should be sited away from the door and, as they are thermostatically controlled, should be set to operate at a few degrees above the thermostat setting for the heating.

It is a great mistake to allow temperatures to rise excessively before ventilating; far better to anticipate the situation and ventilate early. Ventilation at the greenhouse ridge should in fact open up an area not less then one fifth of the floor area, so it will be readily appreciated that most small greenhouses as bought off the shelf are under-ventilated. If such a purchase is being considered, always ensure that extra ventilators can be obtained. Side ventilators are also important and become less obtrusive when fitted as louvres. Automatic openers are also available for these.

SHADING

Shade is another way of lowering temperatures under glass, and may be required as early as March for shade-loving plants and small seedlings. A high proportion of greenhouse plants benefit from some shading from April until the end of September. It is, of course, only actually wanted when the sun is shining, but it is usual to compromise and create a filtered light that is not too dark on dull days.

Shading on the outside of the greenhouse is the most efficient in terms of lowering temperature and blinds that can be raised and

Primula malacoides, a delightful winter-flowerer for the cool greenhouse

lowered are the ideal. It is possible to have automatic control, but this is particularly expensive. Internal blinds of green-tinted plastic sheeting work reasonably well. An alternative is a white wash shading painted on the glass, which is quite satisfactory, and there is a proprietary product that becomes fairly translucent in dull wet weather. Fine plastic netting designed to give various degrees of shading is also available and, when fixed on a length of wood, can be rolled across the greenhouse roof as required.

The other means of combating excessive heat in summer is by increasing the humidity, damping down paths, benches and even walls. Evaporation has a cooling effect and also helps to create a growing atmosphere. This is discussed in the next chapter.

——— Watering and Humidity ———

WATERING

Watering in the greenhouse is an essential activity about which there is much disagreement. Some plants prefer a constant moisture, while others are believed to prefer to become rather dry before being watered. In practice the majority will adapt fairly readily to any steady regime that does not keep them sodden or allow them to dry out enough to begin to wilt. It is, however, a golden rule when watering by hand either to give enough water to moisten all the soil in the pot or to refrain from watering at all. Clean rain water (except in very large industrial towns) is likely to be better for the more delicate pot plants and may be essential for lime-hating plants if the mains water is very alkaline. It is also an advantage if water can stand in the greenhouse before use in cold weather to take the chill off. However, tap water coming under pressure is highly charged with oxygen which is beneficial and static tanks easily become polluted. It is not always understood that air penetrates between the soil particles and that it is essential to all but bog plants that it should. If water fills all the air spaces in the soil for long, most plants will suffer root damage.

Every beginner wants to know how often to water in terms of days and this is an unanswerable question. The rate at which the soil in a pot dries out is affected by sunshine, temperature, atmospheric moisture, type of compost, and how firmly it is packed. The nature and size of the plants and whether they are growing or resting are other factors, not to mention the material of which the pot is made. The advantage of hand watering is that it can be selective, and success must be based on observation.

Holidays and other absences from home are the bane of the greenhouse enthusiast, and now that automatic watering is so widely practised commercially every amateur should give it serious thought.

There are two main types of watering system that can be fully automated. The first is capillary watering, by which pots standing on damp (capillary) matting or sand draw water from below by capillary attraction. The second method is to water the surface of the soil in each pot by means of an individual nozzle or tube. Such trickle and drip systems need electricity for true automation, whereas capillary systems need only a source of water.

The florists' cyclamen, derived from *C. persicum*, is available in many different colours

It is difficult to give simple general advice about automatic watering, because conditions in each greenhouse and the collection of plants grown vary enormously. Even when a watering method is chosen, the interests and aptitudes of the gardener will affect the result, as in all gardening. Temperatures maintained in winter and the method of heating will also alter the climatic conditions in which the watering takes place. Nevertheless, a general understanding of the principles involved and the equipment available is essential, if the best use is to be made of it.

Those specialising in a single kind of plant or crop are faced with the limited problem of its season of growth and rest, but most amateurs grow a mixed collection of plants in pots as well as raising seedlings in spring.

The average small greenhouse tends to be too hot in summer, poorly ventilated, and with too dry an atmosphere. All forms of automatic watering are likely to improve these conditions, and capillary benches, which add moisture to the air and accommodate the largest number of plants in the smallest area, are particularly suitable.

In winter the problems are different. In many greenhouses a combination of low temperatures with a damp atmosphere and poor air circulation encourages troubles such as botrytis, and unnecessary dampness is to be avoided. As better air circulation is achieved with slatted benches, it would be ideal if each pot stood well clear of its neighbours and was watered individually according to its needs.

Capillary watering

The capillary bench is in many ways the most easily controlled and satisfactory method of automatic watering. A sand bench is constructed where the pots stand on damp sand which is 2 in. (5 cm) above the water-level. The valuable aspect of this system is that each pot plant standing on damp sand absorbs from below, by capillary attraction, only the amount of water it uses. So long as the bench has a controlled and constant water level, sudden changes in the weather and the water needs of the plants are catered for. As there is never a shortage of water, the plants grow steadily and fast.

There is a limit to the height of the pot that can be used when watering by this method. The capillary attraction only carries the water up about 5 in. (12.5 cm) when the water level is held 1.5 to 2 in. (5 cm) below the surface of the sand, which has been found to be the most satisfactory arrangement for most plants. Pots up to 6 in. (15 cm) high are satisfactory on capillary benches; larger pots are better watered from the top. For a really reliable and effective capillary bench, it is necessary for it to be level ($\pm \frac{1}{8}$ in.; 3 mm) and to have a controlled, constant water level. It is possible to cover capillary benches with plastic sheeting with a hole for each pot if one is seriously concerned to reduce atmospheric humidity, but I have never found any need for this. Plants that need to be kept dry when resting are, of course, removed from the bench.

On all forms of capillary bench there must be direct contact between the damp surface of the bench and the compost in the pots: there should be no drainage material in the bottom of the pots. Modern plastic pots do not need this anyway. If clay pots are used, a small piece of glass-fibre insulating material can be inserted into the drainage hole to act as a wick. To establish capillarity, pots put on the bench are pressed firmly on to the sand with a slight twisting action. In hot weather if there is any doubt whether capillarity has been achieved, water once from above.

The compost used on all kinds of capillary bench must be well aerated if the plants are to thrive. This means that all potting is done very lightly – just a tap on the bench and a very light firming with the fingers around the edge when re-potting, but no hard ramming. The expert grower of exhibition plants may complain that this is not the way to grow a fine hardwooded plant, and he

Gerbera jamesonii 'Happipot', a dwarf seed strain which is ideal for the small greenhouse

may be right. All I can say is that a mass of healthy and attractive plants can be grown with ease and success. Opinions differ as to what modifications to make to the compost for plants on capillary benches. I use John Innes composts with a little additional coarse grit or sand. I have also used soil-less composts and mixtures of soil-less and loam-based compost. The one essential is to avoid consolidating the compost and to re-pot if a plant looks sickly for no apparent reason. It is wise to keep newly potted plants off the bench for two or three days, as those with damaged roots do not take kindly to this form of watering.

For a home-made capillary bench all that is required is a level bench that is strong enough to support 2 in. (5 cm) of wet sand and the pots without sagging. A solid edge to the staging is also desirable, and the whole is made waterproof with a single sheet of medium or heavy quality plastic sheeting.

The capillary watering kits sold to amateurs are usually designed for use with capillary matting and many are only used at holiday time. Capillary matting is rather ugly and needs fairly frequent renewal, but it can be made to work well. It is essential to test the system thoroughly before a holiday as, if things go wrong, the matting dries very quickly.

The water level can be controlled in various ways. The ordinary domestic ball-cock is a rather rough instrument for making a sensitive response to very small demands for water. There are small plastic floats as used in the self-filling individual drinking bowls designed for cattle. These do not need mains water pressure to work and the amateur plumber can fit them up. If benches are of differing heights, each level will need a separate water control consisting of one of these floats in a plastic box with a plastic tube from the water supply and another to the bottom of the bench. A tiny hole can be made in the plastic sheeting at the base of the bench and small black plastic tubing pushed gently through it, to give a waterproof joint.

Do not use transparent plastic piping as algae will grow inside it and block it in hot weather. For the same reason, light coloured tanks are also a mistake. Algae will also grow on the matting. This does not matter but is ugly. The matting can be washed or treated with chemicals. In time algae and moss will grow on the sand, and chemicals are sometimes used to prevent this. I prefer to scrape off and replace the surface of the sand occasionally. Alternatively, all of the sand can be washed and then replaced. Coarse sand can be obtained in plastic sacks from builders' merchants, DIY stores and some garden centres.

With capillary watering, no matter what equipment is used, one does want to be able to see at a glance whether the apparatus is working. When buying any automated equipment always ask the question: 'How do I see instantly if it has stopped working?'

If it is impossible to achieve a really level surface, one can have an irrigated capillary bench. This consists of a sand-covered bench which is kept watered but is not waterproof at the edges, so that surplus water drains away. A capillary mat can also be used in this way. It is merely a way of adding to the humidity and lessening the individual watering. Capillarity is easily lost in hot weather and it does not have the reliability or usefulness of the controlled capillary bench.

Point watering

There are a number of watering systems that bring water to each plant, either trickling out of adjustable nozzles or dripping from fine tubing. With these the plants may be potted in the traditional ways and the pots can stand on any freely draining staging. Trickle lines and seep-hose can also be used to water plants growing in the ground and to keep irrigated benches moist. When used on the ground a point to remember is that, although long periods of watering penetrate more deeply, a wider area of soil is dampened by more frequent watering for shorter periods.

The pendant flowers of *Kalanchoe manginii* look best in a hanging basket

There is a variety of drip-watering arrangements using very small-bore plastic tubing with individual tubes to each pot; these are supplied by larger-bore rigid tubing. They can have adjustable rates of drip for different plants and positions, and can be tailored to suit any pot arrangement, although an artistic arrangement of plants is made more difficult. With fine tubing the trouble to watch for is blockage of small tubes from lime in the water. These systems are often activated by turning on a tap for a time each day. To automate drip systems, high-pressure water and also electricity are desirable, but amateur kits are available using a simple syphon system. In these, water drips slowly into a small tank, which, when full, empties through the trickle or drip lines connected to it. The disadvantage of this system is that a slow drip, if left unattended for long, is apt to stop completely, while a rapid drip will give too much water.

A sophisticated system using an electric solar control, which adjusts the watering according to the weather, is available for controlling either watering or mist propagation but this is a costly solution.

Perhaps the most obvious way to water plants automatically is to imitate rain, and this is done through nozzles of a similar type to those used for mist propagation. All effective systems of this kind need a source of water at mains pressure or a special pump. In hard water districts continual spraying will leave an ugly lime deposit on both plants and greenhouse glass which is difficult to remove. Where plants needing high humidity are grown, automatic spraying may be used for damping down the floor.

Those who want to specialise in lime-hating plants in districts with very alkaline water must remember that, unless they have ample supplies of rain water, or are prepared for the considerable cost of treating the water, their plants may suffer on an automated watering system.

Electric watering systems

The more elaborate automatic watering schemes use electricity. If both water and electricity are available, there is virtually no watering problem that cannot be solved at a price. The simplest arrangement that works reliably in one's own circumstances is usually the best. One thing to bear in mind is that there is no equipment for controlling the flow of water on a small scale which it is beyond the wit of ordinary people to understand. What is happening may be boxed in or obscured by technical terms, but it is bound to be based on some fairly simple principle. This can be understood and will be explained to those determined to know. Watering arrangements once installed must remain in working order for long periods, and it is virtually impossible to keep equipment working continuously if one does not understand it. Before installing anything that might need professional servicing, it is wise to check whether this is available as well as its likely cost.

Several methods of adjusting the frequency of watering to the weather have been used with varying success. A time clock can be altered to match the season and can operate on a less than daily basis in winter, but it takes no account of whether the sun is shining or not. A solar control using a photo-electric cell has been used with success for some years. It needs to be fixed facing due south and is then activated by the amount of light falling on it. This does not necessarily match up precisely to the amount of water needed, but it is adjustable.

To turn water on and off solenoid (magnetic) valves have long been used, together with a time clock or other electronic controller. A daily watering of not less than 15 or 20 minutes can be arranged by using an ordinary time clock (as used in domestic central heating systems) together with a solenoid valve. If a very short watering time is needed, it becomes more complicated and expensive because a second time clock is necessary. The first

Calceolarias growing in the glasshouses at Wisley

(24 hour) time clock is set to come on for 1 hour a day and to switch
on a second (1 hour) time clock which may be set for as little as 2 or
3 minutes. All this can work off mains electricity, but as it is
considered safer in greenhouses to use low voltages, the electronic
controllers designed for horticultural use usually have a trans-
former and work at 24 volts. These are linked to low-voltage
solenoid valves. It is possible to have solenoids for all the various
couplings of high and low voltage and water pressure, but one must
be sure of what is needed. Obviously it is possible to bring the
silicon chip into play and the day may come when the gardener
presses a few keys by the bedside to activate all systems.

HUMIDITY

Many of us as children have watched the sluicing down of paths
and the spraying of foliage in some large public or private greenhouse. Indeed the warm green smell of damp soil and the mingled
scents of growing plants is what the words greenhouse and
conservatory conjure up in our minds. This is the good growing
atmosphere gardeners talk about. The amount of moisture in the
air, and hence coolness in warm weather, is much influenced by
the amount of green growth within the greenhouse. If there is a

155

concrete floor and a few rather dry pot plants, the temperature will rise very rapidly and the air will be far too dry.

Many gardeners are able and willing to water by hand, using either a watering can or hose. The best can is one with a long spout to facilitate reaching between plants. Hoses may be fitted with trigger-controlled lances and these too make for ease of operation.

The lavish use of hoses is hardly appropriate in the small green-house, but in summer there is a great need to increase the humidity in the air as well as to cool it. Some compromise needs to be made between what is desirable and what is practical. Spraying the floor morning and evening in the summer months is one way out, but the effect is not lasting in hot sunny weather and a more frequent automated spraying would be better. For many plants, shade as well as humidity will be necessary, particularly if the ventilation is poor.

From October to March no extra dampness is needed, and in cool conditions the less water that is splashed about the better. In winter, hand watering should be done early in the day. The human senses are adept at judging atmospheric humidity once they know what is wanted. People tend to feel uncomfortable when the humidity falls below 50 per cent, and this is too dry for plants. A daytime atmospheric humidity around 60 to 65 per cent seems to be satisfactory for most plants. The humidity at night will be and should be higher.

Although mist propagation is not strictly what is meant by watering, I mention it here because it is a useful tool for those who have to be away a great deal. As well as rooting the more difficult cuttings, seeds can be raised to the pricking out stage under mist, and the plants then put on capillary benches.

In mist propagation various forms of so-called 'electronic leaf' are used to control the amount of misting. Perhaps the simplest of these is the one directly linked with the actual conditions of humidity. In this the weight of water falling as mist turns off the system, until the plastic foam sponge which has absorbed the water dries out enough to alter a weight balance and thus turns on the mist once more. The other electronic leaves depend on water connecting electrodes and then breaking the current as they dry out. These may need frequent cleaning if the water is limy. A good alternative is the solar control already described.

Soils and Feeding

SOILS

A simple way to start growing pot plants is to buy a bag of ready-made compost and use it straight from the bag. Today, the choice is bewildering and ever changing, as the combination of research and marketing soon establishes new composts if they prove useful in nursery practice. These are mainly for the production of young plants, which is also what many amateurs are engaged in. However, the more permanent or specimen pot plant still responds to a traditional diet and each one of us will adhere to methods found successful in our own conditions.

Good John Innes compost is as good as it ever was, but unfortunately it becomes rarer every day. The composts are based on a medium loam soil, which only exists in a limited area of the country and is in very short supply. Before being used for potting, turves from good pasture are supposed to be stacked for some months with an even scarcer commodity, strawy manure, and then the whole heap mixed together and screened before being sterilised. Quite apart from the labour involved, the cost of transporting such heavy materials from one part of the country to another has become uneconomic. The result is that much of the John Innes compost sold is made with unsuitable soil. It may also be difficult to find suitable loam to make up one's own compost. However, if the soil is going to be less than ideal anyway, the home-made compost may be preferable for those who have the time and inclination to prepare it.

The loam should pass through a $\frac{3}{8}$ in. (6–7 mm) sieve and must be sterilised. This means bringing it up to a temperature of 82°C (180°F) and maintaining it there for twenty minutes either in a special steriliser or a saucepan over hot water.

To make John Innes seed compost, 2 parts loam, 1 part granulated peat and 1 part coarse sand (all by bulk) are mixed together, with the addition of $1\frac{1}{2}$ oz (40 g) superphosphate of lime and $\frac{3}{4}$ oz (20 g) of either finely ground chalk or limestone. These ingredients need thorough mixing.

The proportions for making John Innes potting composts are 7 parts loam, 3 parts peat and 2 parts sand. To this is added 4 oz (115 g) John Innes Base Fertilizer per bushel for the No. 1 compost, 8 oz (225 g) per bushel for No. 2, and 12 oz (340 g) for No. 3. Ground chalk or limestone is also added to the potting soils at the rate of $\frac{3}{4}$ oz (20 g) per bushel for No. 1 compost (for very young plants), $1\frac{1}{2}$ oz (40 g) for the No. 2 compost (for most plants), and 3 oz (85 g) for the No. 3 compost (which is needed for strong growing plants in large pots or tubs).

There are now some ready-made composts which are of the John Innes type but use modern slow-release fertilizers. These are sometimes in a separate sachet which enables the compost to be stored for longer without deteriorating. All loam-based composts are best used fresh. Another development is the substitution of perlite for the coarse grit or sand in the traditional mixtures. This may not be better but is certainly lighter in weight, which can be important.

A point the manufacturers seem to have overlooked is that keen gardeners like to experiment and mix their own composts. This may upset the scientist's careful formulae, but many amateurs mix ready-made soil-based and soil-less composts together. A half and half mixture is popular and goes some way towards correcting the tendency of plants in peat to become top-heavy.

During the last twenty years there has been a steady increase in the use of peat-based composts. More recently, because of the conservation issue raised by the exploitation of peat bogs, a range of potting composts has been developed based on peat substitutes such as coconut fibre or coir. Like peat, these do not need to be

Mixed tuberous begonias on a greenhouse bench

Spring bulbs like *Iris reticulata* and *Narcissus* 'Tête-à-Tête' will flower earlier in a cold greenhouse

---

sterilised and they can be stored without changing their character, unlike soil. It is an advantage of the manufactured composts, or substrates as they are sometimes called, that they are lighter in weight and more uniform than anything containing soil. Nevertheless, they are not suitable for large specimen plants and the watering technique is different from that in soil-based composts. Peat holds more water than soil but dries out more quickly, as does coir, and once dry may be difficult to wet. Most bought pot plants are in some type of soil-less compost and their care is familiar to many. As the distribution of the various composts is not evenly spread over the country, amateurs need to become accustomed to one or more that are readily available locally. Pine bark and plastic waste are other materials used in some composts.

It is important to remember that plants grown in soil-less composts need supplementary feeding sooner than those grown in soil-based composts, as they do not have the natural reserve of plant nutrients found in soil. The modern slow-release and chelated fertilizers are suited to soil-less composts and have often been included in their composition.

Hippeastrum 'Apple Blossom' is one of several named forms of the very popular "amaryllis"

A potting shed can be regarded either as a necessity or a luxury depending on circumstances, but obviously it is undesirable to store composts, fertilizers, pesticides or unwashed pots in the greenhouse. Where there are children, a locked cupboard for all garden chemicals, away from heat, frost or food, is much more important than a potting shed.

The basic ingredients of all potting composts have been loam, sand, leafmould and well-rotted manure. Each of these is a variable substance, and it is only with experience that one comes to know the feel of a compost that is porous and open, and yet with sufficient humus to retain moisture and nutrition and to support healthy growth. Both the plants grown and the watering methods determine the most effective compost.

Loam

Fibrous loam, the basis of all traditional potting mixtures, is not just garden soil but the top 4 or 5 in. (10–12.5 cm) of well grazed pasture, which has been stacked for a year until the grass has rotted, leaving the fibrous soil. For making John Innes composts it is suggested that a 2 in. (5 cm) layer of manure should be spread on every second layer of turves with a sprinkling of ground limestone on the alternate layers. The whole heap should be wet right through and then protected from heavy rain and left to rot down.

Leafmould
This vital ingredient went out of fashion for a while, but is now a valuable peat substitute. The most dedicated gardeners have never abandoned leafmould if they have a source of supply. It is the product of the decay of leaves of deciduous trees, preferably beech and oak. If collected in autumn and turned once or twice, they break down in about eighteen months into a light fluffy substance that can be passed through a $\frac{1}{2}$ in. (1 cm) sieve. If just left lying in a wired enclosure, leaves usually take two years to decay sufficiently. It must be remembered that there will be lime in leaf-mould from trees on limy soil. Lime-free leafmould is a useful potting material for lime-hating and shrubby plants.

Peat and coconut fibre or coir
Peat does not contain plant food but coir has some nutrient value.

Sand
Sand should be coarse, clean and lime-free. Soft yellow builder's sand is not suitable for potting, nor is sea sand unless very thoroughly washed to remove salt. The sand particles should be up to $\frac{1}{8}$ in. size (3 mm).

Vermiculite
This substance is extremely light and absorbent. In a granulated

Streptosolen jamesonii, a semi-climbing shrub which does not get out of hand, is ideal for a small conservatory

form mixed with peat and fertilizers it forms one of the commercial composts. It is also available as a sterile medium without nutrients. Cuttings can be rooted in it or in a mixture of peat and vermiculite. It is so light that young plants can be lifted from it without damaging the finest roots.

Perlite

This is also a light and absorbent substance created by the heat treatment of volcanic rock. It can be used in a similar manner to vermiculite and is also used in orchid composts, sometimes being substituted for the grit or sand in John Innes type composts. It is available in a variety of granule sizes for different purposes.

Wood ashes

These should be kept dry until used. They are an organic source of potash and are sometimes added to composts, particularly if the soil is heavy.

Lime

Lime is not a fertilizer in the usual sense, although it supplies calcium which many plants need. It improves the texture of clay soils and corrects acidity, but it should not be applied to soil with a pH of 6.5 or above, (pH is a measure of acidity). The neutral point is pH 7.0. Above is alkaline and below acid. A pH of 6.3 is considered best for John Innes compost and pH 5.3 to 5.5 for peat and sand composts. For lime-hating plants the pH needs to be below 6.0. One can discover the pH of the soil with a simple soil testing outfit. One can also ignore the whole thing and hope it is all right!

Manure

Cow manure is perhaps the most generally satisfactory for horticultural purposes, if obtainable, but horse manure is good for heating up a slow compost heap. Poultry manure is chemically rich unless it has been spoilt by exposure to the weather. It should be stored dry under cover. No manure should be used in a greenhouse border until it is in a well-rotted state.

Fish meal

This is an organic source of nitrogen, phosphorus and potash and is a useful fertilizer for the greenhouse border.

Bonemeal

This slow-acting fertilizer, containing phosphorus and a little nitrogen, suffered an eclipse owing to the fear of its transmitting disease, but is now always heat treated.

FEEDING

When plants are growing strongly and the pots are full of roots, the question of additional feeding arises. Some understanding of the processes of plant growth is helpful. We all realise that air, water, light and sufficient warmth must be supplied for growth to take place. Then the leaves will be able to manufacture sugars, starches and proteins, while the roots obtain the various essential minerals and moisture from the soil. Nitrogen, phosphates and potassium, sometimes cryptically referred to as NPK, are the most used and most likely to need replacement. They are present in various proportions in all the compound fertilizers and liquid feeds. Those designed for foliage plants will have more nitrogen, whereas those intended for quick growing flowering plants will have more phosphates and those for tomatoes more potassium. A tomato fertilizer is a convenient source of potash for the occasional feeding of most plants. A frequent error of amateurs is to confine themselves to one liquid feed meant for foliage house plants and then to be amazed when flowering is disappointing.

The precise and detailed needs of many plants are not known, and until recently the essential trace elements found in natural soils could not be included in fertilizers or composts. Now the dedicated gardener can use slow-release fertilizers and many trace elements fused into microscopic glass pellets, and these are even to be found in some commercial composts. Another possibility is the foliar feed whereby plants absorb nutrients through their leaves when sprayed with the diluted feed. This is a quick pick-me-up when things have gone wrong and a sickly plant whose root action is not good can often be encouraged to grow away strongly by foliar feeding.

The secret of feeding is to give little and often and never more than is suggested on the packet. Plants that are resting do not need feeding.

Plants from Seed

Sowing tiny seeds and watching the whole process develop, no matter how long it takes, is a never-ending pleasure to those who become deeply involved in gardening. At the same time there is nothing more maddening than careful sowing, a long wait, and then no results. Many of us will never attempt to acquire the right mental attitude to raise rare shrubs or difficult alpines from seed. But there is room for all tastes in the greenhouse and a wide variety of reliable seeds will give rapid and predictable results with reasonable care. Some plants regarded as difficult are in fact easy, if one can sow fresher seed than is often available in a packet. The length of time seed remains viable is extremely varied and greatly affected by the way it is kept. Although one is advised not to discard pans of rare seeds for two or three years, this is unpractical and depressing in the average small greenhouse.

The equipment used for seed sowing under glass ranges from the fast disappearing clay seed pan and wooden box through plastic trays, pots, pans and other modules to compressed soil blocks, as well as the plastic cast-offs of modern living. Every amateur evolves a personal method, but all successful arrangements ensure a temperature sufficient to allow germination and moisture that is constant without being excessive. It is sometimes said that the ideal temperature for germination of seeds is 5.6°C (10°F) above the optimum growing temperature of the plant concerned. This is only a very rough guide and one cannot give each packet of seed a different temperature. As 21°C (70°F) is satisfactory for the germination of a great many seeds of greenhouse and bedding plants, most seed raisers are designed to raise the temperature to this level. The simpler types lift the temperature but do not have thermostatic control, so that one must guard against the sun shining on them. The most elaborate kinds with both soil and air heating on separate thermostats are very costly. However, soil warming cables can be put into benches or frames and there are many ways of arranging a warm corner in a cooler greenhouse. The highest temperature is only required until the seeds germinate. All seeds need to be sown much more thinly than comes naturally, with the smallest ones merely pressed lightly into the surface and the larger ones buried to their own depth in the compost.

The traditional way of covering seed boxes is a sheet of glass and

Abutilon hybrids (left) may be raised from seed or cuttings; *Campanula fragilis* (right) is very similar to the better-known *C. isophylla*

a sheet of brown paper or newspaper. However, the glass has to be turned each day to remove condensation. An alternative covering is black polythene or bubble plastic sheeting or, better still, several layers of hessian or similar material, which should be kept well moistened. Many propagating cases have rigid plastic covers and only need shading from sunlight. No matter how the seeds are covered, daily inspection is advisable since they must have good light as soon as they germinate. A few plants, including *Primula obconica* and *P. sinensis*, germinate best in light and some do so only in the dark.

Choose a container for sowing in commensurate in size with the quantity of seed available and the number of seedlings required. Too large a receptacle is wasteful of space in a seed-raiser or on a greenhouse bench and uses unnecessary compost. The moment any seedlings appear, they should be moved to stronger light and cooler conditions. They must never dry out or be allowed to stop growing; therefore early pricking out is usually advised. This is always a matter of judgement if the weather is bad and the temperature low, but crowding does weaken growth.

Most plants are pricked out into larger, deeper trays about 2 in. (5 cm) apart in a slightly richer compost. These are easier to keep evenly moist by hand watering than individual small pots. However, if one does not want enough plants to fill the boxes, individual plastic pots may be better, particularly on capillary benches. Quantities of seedlings urgently needing pricking out at the same moment are one of the nightmares of gardening.

Overleaf are some suggestions for plants to grow from seed for greenhouse decoration with sowing dates and the approximate time taken to flower.

Table: plants from seed
A = annual, B = biennial, P = perennial;
MWT = minimum winter temperature

Name	Sowing date; time taken to flower; MWT
Abutilon × *hybridum*. P.	Spring 16 weeks. 7°C (45°F). (See p. 165.)
Alonsoa warscewiczii. P, grown as A.	March to May. 16 weeks.
Asparagus densiflorus 'Myers' (*A. myersii*) and 'Sprengeri' (*A. sprengeri*). P.	Spring. Foliage plants. 7°C (45°F).
Begonia semperflorens. P.	February or March. 6 months. 10°C (50°F).
Browallia speciosa. P.	March or June. 6 months. 10°C (50°F) for winter flowers.
Calceolaria. A and P.	June for flowering following spring. MWT 7°C (45°F). (See p. 155.)
Campanula fragilis and *C. isophylla* P. Trailing	Spring. 16 weeks. 4°C (40°F). (See p. 165.)
Celosia cristata. A.	March. 20 weeks.
Cineraria. See Senecio.	
Coleus (Solenostemon). P, grown as A.	Early spring in heat. Foliage plant. Discard autumn. (See p. 138.)
Cuphea. A and P.	March. 16 weeks. 7°C (45°F).
Cyclamen. P.	June to August. 15 or 16 months. 7°C (45°F). Also F_1 hybrids from March sowing to flower November onwards. (See p. 149.)
Didiscus caerulea. A.	Spring. 18 weeks.
Eccremocarpus scaber. P. Climber.	Early spring for flower same year. (4°C) (49°F).
Exacum affine. B.	March to June for flowering August to December. At least 19°C (50°F).
Freesia. P.	April to June. 7 months. 7°C (45°F).
Gerbera jamesonii. P.	March or when new seed available. 15 months for tall kinds but new compact hybrids flower same year. 10°C (50°F) for reliable winter flowering. (See p. 151.)
Gilia rubra. B.	Early spring for late summer and autumn or July to over-winter and flower next year. 7°C (45°F).
Grevillea robusta. P.	March. Foliage plant. 7°C (45°F). (See p. 176.)
Heliotropium peruvianum. P.	March. 15 weeks.
Hypoestes phyllostachya (*H. sanguinolenta*). P.	Foliage and house plant. 16°C (60°F). (See p. 168.)
Impatiens. A. and P, grown as A.	Spring in warmth. 11 weeks. 10°C (50°F).
Limonium suworowii. A.	Early spring for summer flowering.

Name	Sowing date; time taken to flower; MWT
Lobelia tenuior. A.	Spring for summer and summer for winter in cool greenhouse.
Nemesia strumosa. A.	March to June. 13 weeks. (See p. 168.)
Nierembergia hippomanica (*N. caerulea*) P.	March and April for late summer. Frost-free.
Pelargonium hybrids. P.	January on. 4 to 5 months according to temperature. 7°C (45°F)
Petunia. P, grown as A.	April. 14 weeks.
Plumbago auriculata (*P. capensis*). P. Climber.	Spring. 18 months. 4°C (40°F). (See p. 00.)
Primula vulgaris (modern hybrids) and *P. auricula.*	March to May. For winter and spring in unheated and frost-free greenhouse.
Primula × *kewensis*, *P. malacoides*, *P. obconica* and *P. sinensis.*	May to June for winter. 4°C (40°F). (See pp. 147 and 168.)
Punica granatum 'Nana'. P.	Spring for autumn. Frost-free.
Rehmannia angulata. P.	May for following year. Frost-free.
Salpiglossis sinuata. A.	March and April. 20 weeks. Or August for May in slight heat. (See p. 168.)
Schizanthus pinnatus hybrids. A.	August for April and May, spring for summer. Frost-free. (See p. 134.)
Senecio × *hybridus.* B.	May to July for November to March. 7°C (45°F).
Streptocarpus. P.	February or March in warmth for midsummer. 10°C (50°F).
Thunbergia alata. A. Trailing or climber.	Late March. 15 weeks. (See p. 00.)
Torenia fournieri. A.	March and April. 15 weeks.
Trachelium caeruleum. P.	Early spring. 23 weeks. Or June for next year. 7°C (45°F).

167

Above: *Hypoestes phyllostachya*, the polka dot plant, (left) needs warm conditions; the brightly coloured nemesia (right) is a half-hardy annual
Below: Modern forms of *Primula obconica* (left) come in a wide range of colours; the striking salpiglossis (right) can be fully appreciated in a greenhouse

Plants from Cuttings

The greenhouse favourites grown from cuttings are in themselves enough to keep every greenhouse full of bloom all the year round, as well as providing a special hobby for a wide variety of people.

The actual process of taking cuttings has been revolutionised in recent years for the less skilled. Hormone rooting powders hasten rooting and make difficult species easier to strike, while the plastic bag has created a simple way of ensuring a moist environment for a potful of cuttings until rooting takes place. Mist propagation is a sophisticated option, but it is a luxury for those who do not need to raise many plants.

In general terms it is the vigorous young shoot, which has not yet reached the point of flowering or ripened its wood, that roots most readily. There are green tip cuttings, semi-ripe cuttings and hardwood cuttings, as well as leaf and root cuttings, but the favourite greenhouse plants in this chapter are increased by young shoots. These need to be neatly severed, with a sharp knife or razor blade, just beneath the node or joint and put into their rooting medium while still crisp and fresh.

The compost for cuttings should hold moisture yet drain freely, and there are many alternatives. A good formula is 1 part loam, 2 parts granulated peat and 3 parts coarse sand, all measured by bulk. Peat and sand in equal proportions is a much favoured mixture, while peat and sand, vermiculite or perlite are often used. Peat substitutes may also be used. Under mist pure sand is satisfactory, and it can be used without mist so long as it never dries. For cuttings that are not going to be potted up separately as soon as they have rooted, equal parts of loam, peat and sand provide more nutriment; and equal quantities of John Innes potting compost and sand is yet another alternative.

In any case the moisture of air and soil round the cuttings must never fail before they are rooted. Then they are gradually exposed to the air, first by opening and subsequently by removing the plastic bag or other covering.

In order to create enough plants for a group of ground cover in the garden, and for the replacement of tender shrubs liable to be killed in a hard winter, some propagation is essential. Also, kind friends offer cuttings, and the keen gardener is always ready with a plastic bag so these gifts can be taken home without their wilting.

With perpetual-flowering carnations, removal of smaller side buds results in quality blooms

A majority of greenhouse plants are propagated from cuttings, and there are four favourites which for many are the principal purpose and pleasure of a greenhouse.

Perpetual flowering carnations are still very popular with many gardeners. The necessity here is to have healthy virus-free plants and not to keep them for more than two years. There are specialist nurserymen raising virus-free stock; they will often give advice to the beginner. Little heat is needed, but plenty of air and good winter light are essential. There needs to be room for the plants to grow tall, and red spider mite must be effectively controlled. A minimum winter temperature of 7°C (45°F) is desirable, as winter is the principal flowering season and cut flowers the main purpose. Cuttings can be rooted from November to March, and spring is the time to buy rooted cuttings to start a collection.

Chrysanthemums are the favourite flower of countless enthusiasts in temperate climates, as well as a major horticultural and artistic preoccupation in Japan. There is a good basis for such universal acclaim, for not only is there a great variety of flower size and type from which to choose but a spectacular response to skilled cultivation and training. Chrysanthemums also brighten the dark days of our autumn and early winter and provide exotic forms for flower arrangement.

Clearing out the greenhouse completely in summer and replacing the large plants with fresh young cuttings full of promise each spring are two aspects of chrysanthemum growing that appeal to many. Cuttings root at 7°C (45°C) and high temperatures are never needed. Healthy stock is important here too. (See also the Wisley Handbook, *Chrysanthemums and Dahlias*.)

The fuchsia is no less adaptable in the variety of ways in which it can be trained and grown and also responds to skill in cultivation. It naturally has a very long flowering season and cuttings strike easily at almost any time of year.

Where there is little heat or space, fuchsias can be overwintered by allowing them to become dormant in autumn, when watering is gradually reduced so that leaves fall and the wood ripens. They can take three to four months complete rest, but the root ball should be neither frozen nor dust dry during this time. They are then cut back and started into growth in February or March. Autumn cuttings, or

A Cascade chrysanthemum trained as a standard

young plants being grown as standards, have to be kept growing through the winter, for which a temperature of at least 7 °C (45 °F) is needed and 10 °C (50 °F) is preferred.

Again skill in cultivation brings great rewards. A poorly grown fuchsia is a poor thing indeed. A neutral or lime-free soil, and plenty of judicious feeding, and well-timed training are essential for real success. The plants are attractive to whitefly but otherwise trouble-free. A constant stream of new cultivars, as well as the very large selection of established varieties, means that there is an overwhelming choice. (See also the Wisley Handbook, *Fuchsias*.)

Perhaps the most universal favourite of the unskilled as well as the specialist is the zonal pelargonium (incorrectly known as geranium). The flow of new cultivars continues unabated, with special emphasis on dwarf, miniature and ivy-leaved kinds. The regal or show pelargoniums, flowering mainly from April to June, can be huge bushy plants with magnificent velvety flowers for the decoration of spacious places. Fortunately even more floriferous and adaptable dwarf regals have been created and there are a few miniatures. But all can be grown to a modest size, if confined to fairly small pots and renewed yearly from cuttings.

Zonal pelargoniums have been produced in such enormous numbers and brilliant colours for summer bedding, that not everyone realises the scope of the many kinds which, though they would not make a show in the open in one of our wet summers, are nevertheless good greenhouse and conservatory plants. A visit to a pelargonium nursery can be a revelation. There are even specialists in the miniature forms, and no greenhouse is too small to have a fascinating collection.

In recent years bedding pelargoniums that are raised from seed each year have been so much improved that they are often preferred for municipal bedding. These are usually raised in heat very early in the year and treated with hormone dwarfing agents to encourage early flowers and a better shape. The seed is costly and should have a temperature of 18 °C (65 °F) to germinate. They take much more water than the old geraniums and will not flower before July if conditions are poor. They respond well to automatic watering. All members of this genus are very easily increased by cuttings, which need 7 °C (45 °F) to over-winter happily but survive much abuse.

As with so many plants constantly renewed from cuttings, there is much virus-infected stock, which is why seed-raised plants have become popular, otherwise they are healthy and long-suffering given sufficient ventilation and freedom from frost. The danger of

Many pelargoniums have attractive foliage as well as flowers

spreading virus infection has led the professionals to dispense with the knife when taking cuttings, but amateurs can use discarded razor blades or sterilise the knife between each cutting if there are only a few. Zonal pelargoniums are among the few cuttings best left uncovered for rooting, but as with all cuttings there must be shade from direct sunshine.

To produce a shapely pot plant with plenty of flowering shoots usually requires encouraging the early development of side shoots, and sometimes the prevention of flowering before maturity for the best results. (See also the Wisley Handbook, *Pelargoniums*.)

"Nip out the growing point at 6 in. (15 cm) high" is a frequent instruction in horticulture and could be applied to any of the plants I have mentioned. However, so much thought has been given to the accurate timing of chrysanthemum blooms for show and to disbudding to increase their size, that any serious grower will follow a much more elaborate regime than I could detail here.

The training of woody pot plants is an art that has largely been lost in the last hundred years and can be learnt only by practice and example. In a small greenhouse or conservatory there would be room only for one or two elaborately trained specimen plants, and the emphasis must be on young plants and those that are naturally compact in growth.

Foliage Plants

In the confined space of the small greenhouse all foliage is important. Even flowering plants with large coarse leaves are unlikely to be worth growing. No one should ignore foliage plants, for they are attractive all the year while many flowers only last a short time. They are helpful, too, in avoiding the flat effect of many small pot plants grown on one level, for there are trailers, trees, and palms, as well as the ferns and other shade lovers that grow happily under the staging. Flower arrangers will want trails of foliage to pick, while the strange forms of succulents are also effective in a mixed display. Some coloured leaves are as brilliant as any blossoms, and the cool greys and greens separate and enhance the brighter colours. In a conservatory one is particularly likely to want permanent plants in larger pots.

In the north-facing or otherwise shaded greenhouse, plants grown for their foliage will be the mainstay, but even then the choice will be somewhat limited. It must be remembered that ferns need a damp atmosphere as well as shade. This is difficult to maintain in a small greenhouse or conservatory in summer even with artificial shading, if the structure is in a hot position.

The grey-white *Centaurea cineraria* (left) can be propagated annually from cuttings; the ivy-leaved pelargonium, 'L'Elegante' (right), is well named

The shining green leaves of *Kalanchoe blossfeldiana* are an added attraction to the colourful flowers

The foliage plants now grown as house plants enjoy warmth, but the glass will probably need shading from April to October. Most of them need a minimum winter temperature of at least 10°C (50°F) to do more than endure the winter, but all can be propagated and re-potted and generally encouraged to grow better if there is a greenhouse available in the warmer months. The highly ornamental rex begonias and palms also appreciate shaded warmth in summer. The latter develop slowly and most will survive in the cool greenhouse or conservatory if gradually accustomed to cooler conditions.

Almost everyone seems to have a soft spot for grey leaves. Many such plants are valued in the garden but often lost in our wet winters, so that small plants over-wintered in the greenhouse may serve the double purpose of preserving the stock and providing a useful foil for the brighter colours.

The grey-leaved plants do not want warmth, only freedom from frost and not too rich a soil. The better forms of *Senecio cineraria* and *Centaurea cineraria* are well worth preserving and cuttings can be rooted at the end of the summer. *Helichrysum petiolarum* is another decorative silver plant. *Tanacetum ptarmacaefolium* with silver leaves of a lacy fineness is raised from seed or cuttings. It is at its best in its second year if pruned in March.

Pelargoniums provide a number of coloured leaved and variegated plants. *Pelargonium* 'Lady Plymouth' with finely divided grey and white leaves is a favourite of mine. The cypress-like *P. crispum* 'Variegatum' with small crinkled cream and green foliage and the ivy leaf 'L'Elegante' that is green and white, and pink as well if kept on the dry side, are other suggestions (see p. 174).

Amongst succulents, kalanchoes also provide a choice. *K. marmorata* has blue-grey leaves with brown freckles, while those of the plushy *K. tomentosa* are brown tipped. *Kalanchoe pumila* is a small grey-leaved plant for the front of the staging or a hanging basket. It has pink flowers in spring. These all thrive in 7°C (45°F) and are very easily renewed from cuttings (see pp. 153 and 175).

Asparagus fern is well known and there are several forms. *Asparagus densiflorus* 'Myers' with elegant plumes of foliage is an unusual plant to raise from seed and so is the pink spotted *Hypoestes phyllostachya* (*H. sanguinolenta*) (see p. 168).

For coloured leaves everyone knows Coleus, which can be rapidly grown from seed sown in spring or early summer. Other forms are raised from cuttings and can be grown into larger and finer specimens (see p. 138). In the warm greenhouse or conservatory codiaeums are no less colourful all the year round. Indeed in warmth the choice becomes very large with creepers and climbers, coloured veining and rich velvety surfaces.

Grevillea robusta is a fine foliage plant for a cool greenhouse

Bulbs, Corms and Tubers

Everyone loves bulbous plants in winter and early spring, and few of us fail to be impressed by the showy tuberous begonias or the cyclamen, hippeastrums and gloxinias in their season. Even the less widely grown but no less handsome *Haemanthus, Lachenalia, Nerine* and *Vallota* (*Cyrtanthus*) rouse the greatest enthusiasm when seen in flower. It is the dormant period of the bulbous plant that is its undoing. A bulb, tuber, corm or rhizome is a storage vessel, where the essentials for next year's flowering are kept safely until the favourable season for growth comes round again. Many of the most exotic bulbs from the southern hemisphere adapt fairly readily to a dry period of rest during our winters, instead of enduring a summer drought at home. However, under glass it is up to us to signal the changing seasons and it takes some foresight and an organised approach to grow the more tender bulbs successfully year after year.

Although generally speaking the spring flowering bulbs are planted or re-potted in autumn and the summer flowering ones are planted in spring, some fleshy rooted plants are never wholly dormant and others have a brief rest, which does not fit in with the commercial arrangements for dry bulbs. For those who become interested in the more unusual bulbous plants, there is plenty to learn, quite apart from the possible thrills of travelling to see such plants in their native habitat. The serious collector of rare bulbs often has a bulb frame. This is a raised bed of freely draining soil, which can be protected from the rain or cold at the appropriate seasons for summer ripening or winter dormancy. Here the bulbs can be grouped according to seasonal behaviour and allowed to grow naturally. This method does not create a show of bloom at any one time, but it does allow the best development of the smaller rarer bulbs, the habits of which are sometimes little known. Every bulb has its preferred position in the soil and most will adjust themselves to their natural depth in time, no matter how they are planted.

Although the idea of raising bulbous plants from seed is usually rejected by the beginner, it is not necessarily a slow process. The beautiful *Lilium formosanum* can be flowered in nine months; freesias flower in seven months from a spring sowing and are very easy to grow. The fifteen or sixteen months it can take to raise a

Lachenalia aloides (left) and *Veltheimia bracteata* (right), two unusual bulbous plants for the cool greenhouse

hybrid cyclamen from seed is more exacting, but some of the smaller newer hybrids are very much quicker (see p. 149).

The problem of how to rest a cyclamen corm always provokes conflicting advice, which only goes to show how adaptable fleshy rooted plants are to any steady regime. The secret is to keep them dry but not totally dry, from when the leaves start yellowing until that awkward moment when everyone is on holiday in August and the cyclamen is ready to be re-potted. Do not worry; leave it in the shade outside the back door where the rain will reach it, and you will be reminded to re-pot it on your return.

The small hardy wild cyclamen species, sometimes grown in pans in the unheated greenhouse, can be difficult to start into growth when bought dry and may remain dormant for a year.

Begonias have tiny seeds and need warmth from the time they are sown in January, and it is less demanding to grow them from tubers in spring (see p. 158). The same is true of gloxinias. If they are to be enjoyed again the following year, they must be dried off gradually in October, so that the fleshy roots ripen and the foliage dries off completely before they are stored. They can remain in their pots or be put in dry peat and kept frost free, preferably at a temperature around 10°C (50°F). They are started into growth again in March.

In an unheated greenhouse only the hardy bulbs can be grown in winter, but they will flower several weeks earlier than those in the open. Amongst the smaller hardy bulbs that are attractive in pots in January are the early crocus species and *Iris histrioides* 'Major', followed by the yellow *I. danfordiae* and the scented *I. reticulata* (see p. 159). Another of my favourites is the scarlet multi-flowered *Tulipa praestans*.

'Pink Pearl' (left) is a long-established hyacinth cultivar; the half-hardy *Tigridia pavonia* (right) flowers in early summer

Vallota (*Cyrtanthus*) *speciosa*, or Scarborough Lily, is an evergreen bulbous plant that is shy-flowering until pot-bound and may be difficult to start if sold as a dry bulb. The big scarlet flowers in late summer are worth having. Another evergreen with fleshy roots is *Clivia miniata* and this too can remain in the same pot for years. Its handsome orange or yellow flowers usually appear in late spring.

Perhaps the most spectacular of all glasshouse bulbs are the *Hippeastrum* hybrids (often wrongly called *Amaryllis*) that produce the largest flowers in scarlet, white, pink or orange, to silence the most querulous visitor. They often manage two spikes of four flowers each, although they occasionally miss a year and lose friends that way. Early spring is the planting time, except for those specially prepared for Christmas flowering, which will join the others in blooming in April and May in subsequent years. They need to be gradually induced to rest in September, until they show signs of life in spring. Some obstinately remain evergreen and all need 10°C (50°F) in winter when developing flowers, but are quite happy in cooler conditions once in bloom (see p. 160).

Other fleshy rooted flowering plants to try in the warmer greenhouse or conservatory are *Achimenes*, *Gesneria*, *Gloriosa*, *Haemanthus* and *Smithiantha*. Suggestions for cooler conditions include the winter flowering *Lachenalia*, hybrid nerines flowering in autumn and the handsome *Veltheimia*, which are ornamental through the winter and flower in spring. In an unheated or just frost-free greenhouse, the nearly hardy bulbous plants sometimes grown outdoors are worth considering. These include *Agapanthus*, *Ixia*, *Nerine bowdenii* (see p. 137), *Sparaxis*, *Streptanthera* and *Tigridia*. (See also the Wisley Handbook, *Growing Dwarf Bulbs*.)

Climbers and Shrubs

There is no distinct division between climbers and trailers under glass, or indeed between climbers and shrubs if the latter can be persuaded to cover a wall. In a conservatory climbers give a furnished look and may also be used to give shade. The passion flower (*Passiflora caerulea*) is particularly useful (see p. 187). All climbers and shrubs planted in the ground under glass will have to endure frequent and severe pruning, if they are not to overwhelm the place quite soon.

In a small structure space is so important that one must either confine the roots in a pot or tub or limit oneself to one climber trained up to the roof or back wall. All the favourite conservatory plants are inclined to be rampant. The passion flower can be confined to a tub for a time and pruned hard back in winter. The same is true of the sweet-scented *Jasminum polyanthum* that will root at every joint and grow twelve foot in a season, although young plants blooming in a 5 in. (13 cm) pot look innocent enough. The pale blue *Plumbago auriculata* (*P. capensis*) is a big sprawling shrub with a long flowering season. It is quick and easy from seed or cuttings, takes hard pruning and will even submit to a pot, but cannot really do itself justice that way. There is also a white flowered form (see p. 187).

The Australian blue bell creeper (*Sollya fusiformis*) also has pale blue flowers and grows quickly from seed, but is of modest proportions. The beautiful *Lapageria rosea*, the national flower of Chile, must have a lime-free soil. It is evergreen with small neat leaves, and is slow-growing when confined to a pot. It likes shady cool conditions and the rosy pendant flowers are striking.

There is much to be said for a modest climber that dies back and makes a fresh growth from the root each year. Nature has limited its scope and you do not have to harden your heart and chop it down. *Gloriosa superba* and particularly *G. rothschildiana* is always greatly admired and may reach 6 ft (1.8 m), but is a dry root for half the year.

Tropaeolum tricolorum from Chile is a tuberous rooted climber of moderate vigour that dies down in mid-summer and rests until growth starts again. Light support will be needed for the twining growths wreathed with scarlet and black flowers in spring.

Morning glory (*Ipomoea*) and *Eccremocarpus scaber* are two climbers which are easily raised from seed and come quickly into flower.

The spectacular *Lapageria rosea* carries bell-shaped flowers in summer and autumn

Fuchsias have been mentioned in other chapters and can be trained to any shape, but *F. procumbens* from New Zealand is a curious trailing plant for pots that few would recognise as a fuchsia. The yellow and purple flowers are followed by red berries.

Those with a wall in a sunny conservatory may be attracted by bougainvilleas (see p. 185). If happy, they ramp with thorny branches, but if unhappy they may forget to flower and be covered with greenfly. Plants as diverse as *Begonia fuchsioides* and zonal pelargoniums can be trained against a wall, and the important thing is to choose a plant that is not too attractive to pests. One of these, the orange flowered *Streptosolen jamesonii*, is an amenable bush for training upwards, and its hanging flowers look their best from below (see p. 161).

A group of climbers that are not too thrusting in a small space are the hoyas. Their clustered blossoms look more like wax or icing sugar than any form of plant life. *Hoya bella* is a tricky but beautiful basket plant for the warm greenhouse and *H. carnosa* a less demanding climber in a pot in cool conditions.

Small shrubs in pots often arrive as gifts, such as the Christmas azaleas, and it becomes a matter of pride to keep them from year to year. Plunged outdoors in light shade from June to October and repotted if necessary in April, they can be kept going for years by those who manage never to forget to water them. They should have

7°C (45°F) and a moist atmosphere to bring on the bloom.

The modern poinsettia (*Euphorbia pulcherrima*) is less demanding than its forebears, but prefers a temperature of 13°C (55°F) and regular watering. After a dry and cooler rest in summer, it can be kept for another year, being pruned and repotted when growth starts naturally. It will flower later and the bracts may be smaller, but they are invariably more plentiful.

Hibiscus rosa-sinensis is now a popular house plant that flowers for months but needs 13°C (55°F) in winter.

Camellias are irresistible in flower and valuable in a north-facing cool or cold conservatory. They are best outside in summer as they are hardy plants only needing protection for their winter flowers. (See also the Wisley Handbook, *Camellias*.)

For spring the mimosa best suited in size and slowness of growth to a confined space is *Acacia armata*, with narrow stems of small leaves dotted with little mimosa puffs (see p. 138). The dwarf pomegranate *Punica granatum* 'Nanum' quickly grown from seed to flower at 3 in. (7.5 cm) tall is the nearest thing to a mini shrub designed for the beginner in a mini greenhouse.

Camellias are very successful in a cold or cool greenhouse

Pests and Diseases

PESTS

There are five extremely persistent greenhouse pests that need to be kept under control: vine weevil, mealybugs, red spider mites, whitefly and aphids. For suppliers of biological controls, see p. 69.

Vine weevil
The dull black adult beetles are active at night, eating notches from the leaf margins of many plants. The white grub-like larvae are more important as they feed on roots and corms of most pot plants, often killing them. The adults can be sprayed with pirimiphos-methyl or dusted with HCH. Alternatively, handpick them off by torchlight. The grubs can be controlled by a nematode drench.

Mealybugs
These are first noticed as a patch of white wool – a sign they are breeding. Deal with a small infestation by picking off each insect with a pin or painting the bugs and their eggs with methylated spirits. Heavier infestations can be sprayed with pirimiphos-methyl, malathion or a systemic insecticide. In summer, biological control is possible with the ladybird predator *Cryptolaemus montrouzieri*.

Red spider mites
Hard to spot as the sap-sucking mites can barely be seen without a hand lens. Affected leaves become pallid and when infestations are severe webbing can be seen. The mites revel in hot, dry atmospheres so spray the undersides of leaves with water in warm weather. Apply derris, bifenthrin, pirimiphos-methyl, malathion or dimethoate. Biological control can be effective during summer by introducing the predator *Phytoseiulus persimilis*.

Glasshouse whitefly
The tiny insects rise into the air when plants are disturbed. Both adults and nymphs suck sap and remedies must be applied several times to eradicate this persistent pest. Spray or fumigate plants with permethrin. Less persistent alternatives include insecticidal soaps, bifenthrin, pyrethrum, malathion or pirimiphos-methyl.

Yellow sticky traps can reduce infestations, particularly if plants are shaken regularly. Biological control using the parasite *Encarsia formosa* is effective when daytime temperatures are above 21°C (70°F).

Aphids

Various forms of greenfly, which may also be black, buff or pink, can be dealt with using insecticidal soaps, pyrethrum or derris, or with a systemic insecticide. In summer, hoverfly larvae take a high toll of greenfly and should be encouraged. Predatory midge larvae, *Aphidoletes aphidimyza*, can be purchased for biological control.

Ants

They transport aphids from plant to plant and thereby spread virus diseases. Use beniocarb, permethrin or pirimiphos-methyl dusts or proprietary ant baits around nesting sites to discourage ants from establishing themselves in the greenhouse.

Slugs

These feed mainly at night, making holes in leaves, flowers and stems. Seedlings and cuttings can be severely checked. Handpick by torchlight or scatter slug pellets around affected plants. Use the nematode *Phasmarhabditis hermaphrodita* for biological control.

Leafhoppers

The adults readily jump off the leaf when disturbed; the immature nymphs are less mobile. Both stages suck sap causing a whitish mottling of the leaf surface. Control by the chemicals listed under red spider mite.

Leafminers

The twisting linear tunnels in the leaves spoil the plant's appearance. Remove affected leaves at first sign of attack.

Earwigs

In hot dry summers, earwigs puncture holes in succulent leaves or damage chrysanthemums and other flowers. Trap earwigs in flower pots stuffed with straw or under old sacking or seed boxes.

Scales

These sap suckers hide on the backs of the leaves of oleanders, citrus and other evergreens. Spray the undersides of foliage with malathion or pirimiphos-methyl or hand clean.

Thunbergia gregorii (left) resembles *T. alata*, but does not have the "black eye"; *Bougainvillea glabra* and its forms (right) are the best choice for a cool greenhouse, flowering when quite small

---

Thrips
Blackish grey winged insects up to 2 mm long are hard to find but cause damage similar to that made by red spider mite. They only establish in dry atmospheres so discourage by spraying plants with water.

Sciarid flies
Greyish brown flies run over the compost or fly slowly round pot plants. Their maggot-like larvae live in the compost where they feed on decaying organic material. They may also damage living roots of seedlings and cuttings but will not harm healthy established plants. Yellow sticky traps will trap flies. Protect vulnerable plants by mixing malathion dust in with the compost or water with pirimiphos-methyl.

DISEASES

Damping-off
Several different soil and water-borne fungi cause the collapse of seedlings at soil level. Prevent by using new compost and watering carefully with mains water. Regular applications of a copper fungicide may prevent infection.

Foot rot, crown rot and root rot
A brown or black rot at the stem base, around the crown or at the roots results in wilting or collapse of the top growth. Use new compost, sterilized pots and clean water to prevent infection.

Grey mould (*Botrytis cinerea*)
Leaves, stems and flowers rot and become covered with a grey-brown mass of fungal spores. Most troublesome in greenhouses where humidity is high and hygiene is poor. Prevent by prompt removal of all diseased or dying parts. Ventilate to reduce humidity and water in the morning, not at night. Spray with carbendazim at first signs of infection.

Powdery mildew
White powdery coating on the leaves and sometimes on other parts. Ventilate the greenhouse well and water before the compost dries out completely. Remove severely affected leaves and spray with carbendazim or triforine.

Rusts
Powdery pustules appear on the lower leaf surface producing orange spores on fuchsias and cinerarias, dark brown or buff spores on chrysanthemums and chocolate-coloured spores on pelargoniums and carnations. Remove and destroy affected leaves; in severe cases destroy the plant. Ventilate the greenhouse well and water carefully so droplets do not remain on the foliage. Spray with mancozeb.

Viruses
These can affect a wide range of plants causing mottling, blotching or striping of the leaves with pale green, yellow or black. Leaves may also be distorted and the plants stunted. Destroy any plant showing these symptoms and control aphids, ants and leafhoppers.

Physiological disorders
Caused by unsuitable cultural conditions, the most common disorder is oedema. Pale pimple-like outgrowths appear on the undersides of the leaves and on the stems and they later burst and become brown and powdery or corky. Ivy-leaved pelargoniums are particularly susceptible. Oedema is the result of overwatering and/or too humid an atmosphere. Do not remove affected parts but improve ventilation and water carefully.

Bud drop
Never allow the compost to dry out when flower buds are beginning to develop.

Above: A mixture of begonias, fuchsias and schizanthus gives a brilliant show
Below left: *Passiflora* caerulea, the passion flower, a reliable and almost hardy
climber; *Plumbago auriculata*, right, can be pruned hard in late winter

Corky scab
Corky spots develop into sunken patches on cacti. Ensure plants
are grown in good light, but not burnt by excess sun. Ventilate to
reduce humidity.

Index